Senior Camino

A Guide for Seniors

Walking the Camino de Santiago

Donald Bowes

Contents

	Acknowledgments	
	Preface	
	Introduction	1
1	Getting There	9
2	Getting Ready to Go	11
3	Preparation	17
4	Traveling to *St. Jean Pied de Port*	29
5	*St. Jean Pied de Port* to *Pamplona*	33
6	*Pamplona* to *Logrono*	41
7	*Logrono* to *Burgos*	51
8	*Burgos* to *Fromista*	63
9	*Fromista* to *Sahagun*	71
10	*Sahagun* to *Leon*	77
11	*Leon* to *Rabanal*	87
12	*Rabanal* to *O'Cebreiro*	99
13	*O'Cebreiro* to *Sarria*	117
14	*Sarria* to *Santiago*	127
15	*Santiago de Compostela*	155
16	Going Home	165
	Epilogue	169

Acknowledgments

Walking the *Camino de Santiago* was an experience unlike any other I have ever had in my life. So much of that experience was made inexplicably richer due to the wonderful fellow pilgrims I met along The Way. If I have any regrets, it is that I was not more intentional in making the effort to stay in touch with all of them. As I recall our shared experiences, I am saddened by this fact. I wonder how they are doing now in their lives in Australia, China, Brazil, Denmark, Germany, Finland, Canada, France, Austria, Norway, Mexico, Ireland, England, Switzerland, North Carolina, Ohio, Massachusetts and California. As these great people are woven into the fabric of my story, I have decided to change their names to protect their privacy, since many of our conversations as we walked, ate, and drank together were intensely personal -- more than one might expect after such a short period of time. Fellow pilgrims, you know what I'm talking about.

I am indebted to my Church family at Epiclesis in Carmichael, CA who prayed continually for our safety and well-being. There were definitely times when I could feel those prayers palpably – often when they were most needed.

To my dear friend, Greg Sutter, who accompanied me on the 1st Camino, and who shared every single experience with me, I could not have made the trip all the way without your strong encouragement and good humor. Thanks for the shell you bought for me in *Astorga*.

There were some *Facebook* friends who followed us every step of the way. Their encouraging comments and excessive "likes" were a great support to our effort. Doug, Laurie, Cata, Richard, and Michael thank you so much.

Lastly, I want to recognize my family back home who were so firmly behind my decision to go and who lifted me up every day with prayer and support: my son Dylan and his wife, Nicole, who sent me a great video in the middle of the first Camino that lifted my spirits so; and my wonderful wife, Heather who got me off my butt after my surgery and pushed me to train day after day, and never doubted that I could do this, not once. I love you, sweetheart, and I am so glad we could go back and do the Camino together! Thanks for putting up with me while I have been writing this book. You are my inspiration always.

...Donald Bowes, Fair Oaks, 2017

Preface

"I think that I cannot preserve my health and spirits, unless I spend four hours a day at least – and it is commonly more than that – Sauntering through the woods and over the hills and fields, Absolutely free from all worldly engagements."

...Henry David Thoreau, <u>Walking</u>

"*Pilgrim (parepidemos)* tells us we are people who spend our lives going someplace, going to God, and whose path for getting there is the way, Jesus Christ. We realize that 'this world is not my home' and set out for the 'Father's house.' Abraham, who 'went out,' is our archetype. Jesus, answering Thomas' question, 'Lord, we do not know where you are going; how can we know the way?' gives us directions: 'I am the way, and the truth, and the life; no one comes to the Father, but by me' (John 14:5-6)."

...Eugene H. Peterson, <u>A Long Obedience in the Same Direction</u>

Several years ago, during an annual mission trip to a school in Baja Mexico, I found myself sitting alone on a stone path in the middle of an olive orchard. We had all taken a lunch break from our work, and I sought some quiet time to contemplate my "issues" with God. Principal among these issues was my dissatisfaction with the direction of a church ministry with which I had been involved for many years. I won't go into all the details surrounding all this, but I was beginning to realize deep within me that something regarding this direction had to change -- or perhaps it was me that had to change!

It was a picture perfect day at that moment in the orchard in Mexico. The sky was an incredibly deep blue and cloudless as far as one could see. I gazed down at the path beneath me and realized that someone had fashioned the shape of a cross in the stones--something you would only notice if you intentionally stopped to really look at the path. Sensing the stillness of the moment, and the sound of only the wind gently rustling through the olive trees, I figured this would be a good place and time to cry out to God. The prayer from my heart was "Lord, what is it that you want me to do with my life to serve You? Is what I am doing now to serve you where you want me? Or do you have something else in store for me? Please tell me, Lord! I need to hear from you on this!"

There was, of course, that deafening silence that always seems much longer than it really is – just nothing coming back at me. In the distance, I could hear the sound of the children leaving their homes to go from one activity to another. Realizing that I would soon need to get back to the work I was doing for that day, mixing concrete and pouring it into forms for a patio, I began to get myself back up, but before I could get to my feet, I heard the unmistakable voice of God saying to me, "Be still, and know that I am God." That was it, that's what I heard loud and strong. It was at this 'path along the road' that I began to realize that the sooner I came to the end of myself, the sooner God would be able to take over. I returned from the mission trip shaken with this simple, yet profound, revelation.

Back home in California, as I contemplated what had taken place, I knew that I could no longer continue to operate on my own strength in a ministry with 'impure motives'. Soon after, I stepped down from the ministry leadership role and decided instead to begin to follow Jesus for real. My dear friend, Norm, had a similar experience. He described it as "coming to the realization that for decades in his Christian life, he had been fishing out of the wrong side of the boat."

Thus began a long period of repentance and an amazing time of discipleship and growth for me personally. In the many years that have followed, I find myself just beginning to scratch the surface of what baptism into Christ is all about, how we are new creatures, reconciled to God through the life, death and resurrection of our Lord and Savior. Starting from the middle of that crude stone path in Mexico, I have been walking out this baptism every day of my life. Eugene Peterson states in his wonderful book, *A Long Obedience in the*

Same Direction that Christians cannot, or should not, stay in one place, lest they risk becoming statues. We need to keep moving forward along a path that keeps us ever becoming more like the One we follow, Jesus. This experience is what led me to move from existing as a statue to becoming a pilgrim.

ΑΩ

Introduction

I started my formal education at a small liberal arts college in Pennsylvania. My original goal was to attend law school after graduation, but somewhere in my sophomore year I became somewhat derailed from History and Political Science and gravitated towards the study of Literature. By the time I was a junior, I had changed my major to English, and I had to scramble to catch up with all the required course-work. During this period of intense study, I became enamored by the works of the *Transcendentalists*. Eventually, I crossed paths with the writing of Henry David Thoreau. As an impressionable youth, I was caught up in this 19th century philosophical movement. I learned, as Immanuel Kant had postulated, that in order to understand the nature of reality, one must first examine and analyze the reasoning process that governs the nature of experience. So it seemed logical to me that this philosophy was a reaction to realism. I loved the Romantic notion which surmised that divinity pervades all nature and humanity. Somewhere along the way, I stayed up all night to write an essay on *Walden* which was due at 9:00 am. I only managed to write two pages, but the professor gave me an "A" on the paper, indicating that it was "admirable in the very nature that Thoreau extolled – Economy!" In June 1862, Thoreau published an essay in the *Atlantic Monthly*. It was simply titled, *Walking*. He considered this his best essay. Here is a quote that has seemed entirely suited to our "Camino Experience":

> "...I have met with but one or two persons in the course of my life who understood the art of Walking, that is, of taking walks – who had a genius, so to speak, for SAUNTERING, which word is beautifully derived "from idle people who roved about the country, in the Middle Ages, and asked charity, under pretense of going a la Sainte Terre" to the Holy Land, till the children exclaimed, "There goes a Sainte-Terrer," a Saunterer, a Holy-Lander. They who never go to the Holy Land in their walks as they pretend, are indeed mere idlers and vagabonds; but they who do go there are saunterers in the good sense, such as I mean. Some, however, would derive the word from sans terre without land or a home, which therefore, in the good sense, will mean, having no particular home, but equally at home everywhere. For this is the secret of successful sauntering..."

In the spring of 2012 I attended a one-day seminar that focused on spiritual contemplation while walking. The idea of creating the space to be "alone with my thoughts" or "talking to God in the solitude of a long walk" had great appeal to me. It is my belief, certainly based on my personal experiences, that we are almost always closer to God when we are alone with Him and take the time to pray as well as listen to find out what God has in store for us. At the seminar there were some practical ideas on how to do this which I found very intriguing and well worth pursuing. Returning home, on the evening of that seminar, I happened to watch the movie *The Way*, directed by Emilio Estevez and starring his dad, Martin Sheen. The film tells the story of a sixty-something ophthamologist from California who goes to France to recover the remains of his son who has died there in the mountains, having perished in a snowstorm. After arriving and subsequently having his son cremated, he learns from the local police chief that his son had just started to walk the *Camino de Santiago* when the tragedy occurred. The chief goes on to explain some of the details about the Camino, and the man then decides to make the trip himself in honor of his son. Along the way, the character scatters his son's ashes, learns many things about himself, makes some unlikely friends, and by the end appears to be considerably changed by the experience.

When the movie had finished, I had the strong feeling that I had to take this trip, but I kept that realization to myself for a while until I felt ready to announce it to my wife and friends. From time to time, I have been subject to grandiose ideas that never come to fruition, but this was something profoundly different. It just seemed really clear to me that I needed to do this. A few weeks later, I announced my intentions to walk the Camino the following spring in 2013, in the middle of my 70th year, and that I was going to begin preparing for the trip immediately. I must say that it helped immensely that my wife, Heather, and all my friends were very supportive of this decision, and were more than encouraging all along the way. Little did I know at that point that approximately two years later, I would return to the Camino to walk with Heather from *Leon* to *Santiago!*

What follows in these pages is partially a chronicle of these walks through northern Spain along the *Camino de Santiago,* specifically the *Camino Frances,* and also an encouragement to those over 65 who may be contemplating such a similar endeavor to get going and do it. It is my fondest hope that those who read about my journeys will be spurred to action and know that it is possible to complete the trek with good preparation and careful planning. I was prompted to write this book when I realized that I would have cherished this sort of detailed information that catered to someone my age if it had been available to me when I was entering into my own decision-making process. The movie *The Way* paints a great picture of a literal and figurative journey of one man. The producers of the film were naturally intentional in including some dramatic moments that were a little "over the top" (the backpack falling in the river, the chase through the streets of Burgos) and also leaving out much of the "nitty gritty" details involved with a 500-mile trek across Northern Spain (i.e. blisters, severe weather, etc.) In my opinion, these decisions were appropriate for a 90-minute dramatic film that was, of course, never intended to be a documentary. As a result of that "artistic license," the portrayal lacks a somewhat realistic perspective of the true physical, emotional and spiritual aspects that you can expect to encounter.

My first Camino started in *St. Jean Pied de Port,* France and ended in *Santiago de Compostela,* Spain. This is known as the *Camino Frances,* and it is by far the most popular of the dozen or so Caminos that lead from different parts of Europe and make their way to Santiago. The total walking distance was 816 kilometers (510 miles). It took me 38 days to get from the start to the finish. Three of those days were spent "resting and sightseeing" in large cities along the way: *Pamplona, Burgos,* and *Leon*. I also stayed three nights in *Santiago* at the end, catching my plane early the next morning to connect with the flight home to the US.

The second trip along the *Camino Frances,* started in *Leon* and ended in *Santiago*. This shorter distance of approximately 250 miles was chosen because of the limited time available to my wife, Heather, who only had 3 weeks of allotted vacation. The second Camino took us 17 days to complete and followed a slightly different route in a few sections.

In preparation for my original walk, I found that there were many excellent books in print, guide books, as well as on-line forums about "walking the Camino" all of which contain wonderful tips and information which are indeed helpful to all of us. But, to my knowledge at the time, none of these resources were tailored to the senior citizen. It was only after transcribing my own journals of the trip and recalling the varied experiences from memory that I realized how helpful these tidbits might be to others around my age who were wondering if this would be something they might be able to do. Let's face it: we older folks have some health and fitness issues to consider that we did not even think about 25 years ago. Also, I have found that my own tolerance level towards certain aspects of travel has significantly mellowed or narrowed depending on the circumstances. As an example, I know that in my later years now, I need a good night's sleep in order for me to function well – a big consideration! Maybe there are some of you who find that they need quick access to a bathroom throughout the night, first thing in the morning – whatever!

Within the first few weeks of the planning phase, I made a critical decision that affected not only the cost of the trip, but also the length and timing of the walk itself. Up to this point in my life, I had been on nearly two dozen mission trips to remote places where I had slept, bathed and occupied rather rudimentary quarters with many people at the same time. I was able to do this for many reasons I suppose, not the least of which was that I was able to put my own comfort aside for a brief period while serving the needs of others. Over the years these trips became harder for me due to the simple fact that I was growing older, and it was becoming more essential that I was able to sleep and eat well in order to be an effective servant. On one trip I spent 5 days on the Navajo Nation reservation and slept only about an hour per night! After that experience, I knew that my days of voluntary deprivation were definitely behind me.

Two things are important here. One is that these trips were short in duration, usually one or two weeks at a time. In that respect it was not hard to "put up" with these temporary living conditions simply because they were so short-term. The other thing is that I would not be serving others on my trip to Spain. This was going to be a six-week duration, and each day would be strenuous, to say the least! In order to complete the trip physically, I knew I needed to be attentive to my personal sleep requirements as well as my nutrition requirements.

To this end, I decided to avail myself of a travel service that would book hotels for me along the way and also provide a baggage service that would carry my gear from place to place. This would mean that I would only have to carry enough in a backpack that would meet my needs for the day. Once I decided upon the suitable company that would provide this service, I knew what my budget would be, and I was able to confidently move ahead with the planning and training phase. For the purposes of this book, I will refer to this "travel service" as the "Travel Company".

A word about this decision to all those who may be "on the fence" in this matter. When I first decided to walk the Camino, I was probably in what I would call the "purist camp". My initial thoughts were that I wanted to experience a pilgrimage along these centuries-old paths that would allow me to just go and avail myself of the hospitality of strangers and friends along the way. I struggled with this concept for some time until I began to seriously consider my own personal issues that I have just outlined above. There are many who will tell you that this is the only way to go – that the "true" pilgrim would only do this or that. My advice is to smile and take this as one opinion. There is always validity in approaching your Camino in this manner if this is what you want to do. The reality is that each person has his or her own Camino, and all ways and methods are valid. This reality is borne out when we all reach Santiago, receive the *Compostela,* and go to the Pilgrim's Mass together in the Cathedral. I do not feel less of a pilgrim in any way, shape or form because I stayed in hotels, *pensions, casa rurales* as well as *albergues* along the way. My experiences proved to be rich and extremely rewarding for me, and as a person of advancing age, I was able to truly enjoy every day because I was rested and aware. This was a safe and sane way for me to walk 500+ miles – nothing more and nothing less

Here's another reality to be aware of. If you are intending to just arrive on the Camino and start walking not knowing where you will stay – just leaving that up to chance – great! But be aware that the Camino is becoming increasingly popular. That means that the law of "supply and demand" applies to beds available in the various municipal *albergues* along the way. Almost without exception, those pilgrims who were staying exclusively in the municipal *albergues* were literally up at the crack of dawn to make time to get to the next stopping place by no later than 2pm to ensure that they would have a place to stay for the night. This required a rigorous pace that allowed little stopping along the way. I would say that when I entered a town where my hotel was located at the end of a long day, those same pilgrims were still looking for a place to stay or they were sitting/standing in long lines waiting for a spot to open up. In many cases, their search took them up to two hours, and in some instances, they had to go to the next town, several kilometers away to find a place to lay their head. This was what I had anticipated before going, and a major decision factor for me choosing the Travel Company route. You might consider this a spontaneous adventure, and perhaps it might be, if you had unlimited time to make the trek. I considered it way too fatiguing and annoying for my old bones – especially after walking 15 to 18 miles. There was never a day when I got into a town where I was going to stay that I was not totally relieved to know that I had a private room and a shower waiting for me.

Additionally, there are those who will tell you that to be a true pilgrim, you have to take the entire trip along one of the ways to *Santiago*. For example, if you choose the *Camino Frances* route, you must go all the way from *St Jean Pied de Port* to *Santiago*. Anything less is just a partial Camino. Do not listen to this false narrative. This is another elitist view that you will find the vast majority of pilgrims will reject. That being said, it is true that if it is your goal to earn the *Compostela* in Santiago (an official certification of completion), you must walk at least 100km along the route and have proof of having stopped along the way with *sellos* (stamps) in your *credencial* (pilgrim's passport). On the *Camino Frances* this would mean that you would have to walk the distance from *Sarria* to *Santiago*. I met several fellow pilgrims that were "only" doing a segment of the *Camino Frances* because that is all their time constraints would permit. Some were planning to do multiple segments from year to year until they would eventually complete the entire route. I was privileged to have the ability to complete the entire journey in one trip, being only limited in time by financial restraints. Of course, if you live nearby in Europe, it is easier to return yearly or semi-annually to accomplish this. Coming from the USA, Asia, Australia or Canada is obviously a more expensive proposition.

Another decision that I faced was whether or not to attempt to make the trip by myself. On the first Camino, once it was determined that my wife could not accompany me due to her work schedule, I had to face the fact that I would very likely be on my own. I have travelled extensively by myself all over Europe, so I was prepared to go it alone, thinking that I would surely meet people along the way that I could walk with if I chose to do so. As it turned out, a good friend of mine decided that he wanted to go and we were able to plan our trip together. This was indeed a welcome addition and eliminated any fear of loneliness or isolation that I had felt from time to time before going. Although I thoroughly enjoyed the company of my friend, and he was a great encouragement to me along the way, I am confident that I could have made the trip by myself, certainly after having done it. So, I would encourage anyone to not be afraid of doing the Camino by one's self. There are literally hundreds of fellow pilgrims that you will encounter along the way who will keep you company and provide many hours of great fellowship, should that be your wish. In my experience, the majority of pilgrims I encountered had come to walk the Camino alone. Some had found companions to walk with from time to time, but others continued in solitude because that is what they wanted to do.

I was also surprised to see a large quantity of women walking the Camino by themselves. In general, it is safe on the *Camino Frances* since most of the time you are never really far apart from someone else that a call for help would not be heard. Although I had a friend along with me, we did not always walk at the same pace and got separated often. There were times when I found myself alone for two or three hours at a time, seeing someone else in the distance, whether behind or ahead, only occasionally. Also, there are a few rather secluded sections that I found daunting and a little bit dangerous. So let me just say, at the risk of being politically incorrect, if you are a woman walking alone, I would recommend that you find a companion or group that you trust to walk these sections with you – just because those places are a little "out there!" No one will object to being approached and asked if you could walk with them for a spell because of the remoteness of the trail. By the same token, no one will object if you tell someone who has joined up with you that you would like to walk alone for a while. These are the "unspoken rules" of the Camino. Naturally, some of the larger cities have areas that should not be "experienced" as a single woman, especially at night. But this is the same precaution you would take in any city in the world. Just use your common sense. Find a companion or a small group and go have fun. You will have no trouble doing this.

Chapter One

Getting There

Unless you live in Europe, you will need to fly to the nearest city that will afford you easy connections to whatever starting point you choose. If that starting point is *St. Jean Pied de Port* (SJPP), you cannot fly directly there. Most pilgrims fly to either *Paris, Madrid, or Barcelona* and then make connections by air or train/bus to get to the little town at the foot of the Pyrenees. From most points in the rest of the world, your flight to *Paris* will take you into *Charles de Gaulle* airport (CDG). Then you can fly to *Biarritz* and take a train from there, or you can take a train all the way from *Paris* to *Bayonne* and get a connection from there to SJPP. It is an easy walk from the train station in SJPP to just about anywhere in town and it feels good to stretch your legs to do so.

If you fly to *Madrid*, you can take a bus or train to *Pamplona* and make connections from there via bus or taxi (expensive) to SJPP. Many pilgrims have written about their experiences with an *alberque* in Pamplona (*Corazon Puro*) that will arrange to pick you up at the *Pamplona* stations, take you to the *albergue* for the night's stay, and then drive you to SJPP the following morning. I have heard wonderful compliments about these hosts.

[NOTE: In early 2017, the hosts at *Corazon Puro* announced that they would be temporarily closing their *albergue* for an indefinite period of time.]

Others tell of opportunities they had to share taxis with fellow pilgrims that were far more direct and immediate, costing a fraction of what they would cost if you had taken the taxi alone. Look around, you will spot the other pilgrims without question. You will find they will be anxious to make connections and new friendships and quite willing to share any information they have. This is the beginning of your Camino! Jump in and have fun!

On my second Camino, I took a train from *Madrid* to *Leon*. This was a fairly simple process. It is possible to buy a train ticket ahead of your arrival on-line either directly from the *Renfe* (Spanish train system) or through a service such as *Rome2Rio*. I used *Rome2Rio* and found the group to be quite helpful. You will receive a printout of your official ticket via email. This ticket entitles you to a pass on the *Cercanias* Train (C-1) that leaves Terminal T-4 on a regular basis to *Chamartin* Station. You can catch the *Cercanias* Train on the underground floor of T-4, down the steps on the Arrival level. If you already have a ticket for the C-1 train, there are vending machines that will give you a free ticket to get you through the turnstiles, or you can get a free ticket for the turnstiles at the *Renfe* ticket office on this lower level right opposite the turnstiles. Although the trip from *Barajas* Airport to *Chamartin* is less than 15 minutes, my advice is to leave sufficient time between your arrival in *Madrid* until your train departs from *Chamartin* to accommodate any change of schedule, long custom lines or delays. I think two hours is plenty of time, but I wouldn't suggest making this any tighter. The train takes approximately two and a half hours to get to *Leon* and has two stops along the way. At the small train station in *Leon*, most hotels or albergues are within easy walking distance. There is also a taxi line to the rear of the station. You will find that you are probably not more than 10-minute taxi drive from any place you are staying in *Leon*, except for the *Parador*, which is on the far side of town.

Other starting points may be in such cities as *Burgos* or *Logrono*. I met several pilgrims who were making connections from these cities to *Barcelona* via bus. *Astorga* can easily be accessed by bus from *Leon*. If you have only a week or so and are planning to walk from *Sarria* to *Santiago*, you will most likely fly into *Santiago* and get a bus to *Sarria* or train to *Lugo* and bus or train from there.

A word about travel time. You are undoubtedly aware of your personal travel clock – how your body reacts to time changes and the vicissitudes of 'jet lag'. Depending on where your origination point actually is, and the number of "legs" that may be in your flight plans and arrangements, you may be spending over 24 hours in transit to the starting point of your Camino. This could well be a nine-hour time differential, or perhaps longer should you be coming from Asia. I advise giving yourself at least one "buffer" day to recover from the travel before you walk. This is especially true of walking from SJPP, because the first day is quite demanding physically.

Chapter Two

Getting Ready to Go

Things to Settle on First

I suppose it should go without saying, but there are some very practical things you will need to decide on right at the start so that you can proceed with making plans for your trip. Once you have these items dialed in, you will find that most everything else will fall into place. You will then know what specific gear you need to assemble in order to effectively accomplish your Camino. If you need to purchase new equipment, you will have the time to check out all the various alternatives that are available to you and watch for sales, etc. Most importantly, you will be able to set out a training schedule to ensure that you will be in the appropriate physical shape to walk the distance you have chosen. If you have a fixed amount you can afford to spend on your trip, then that factor may narrow your choices. That's okay. There is plenty to see in a short-term Camino and lots of fun to be had.

When Will You Travel?

There are many options to consider here. Almost all of them revolve around two factors: (a) weather and (b) crowds. Some travelers may also be limited by season due to work and/or vacation schedules, etc. In those cases, you will obviously have to go when you can get away. As a rule, the best weather is generally in the spring or fall, although you will be subject to some rain. The summertime can be quite hot, especially on the *Meseta*, the two to three days after Burgos, but there is less chance of rain. The winter can be hazardous due to severe weather with snow and ice. (Travel on the Camino during the winter is not recommended for the inexperienced.) As far as crowds are concerned, the early spring and late fall are probably the ideal times to travel. The summer will have the greatest crowds due to the fact that most people take their vacations at this time. It you are using a Travel Company, there shouldn't be a problem with finding a room, as long as you are booking well in advance. There will be far more people walking the Camino in the summer however, so it will be very crowded on the trail or wherever you go. Staying in the *albergues* will be an issue during the summer months, requiring patience and adaptation. The fewest crowds will obviously be in the winter months. My personal experience is with the spring and fall.

Springtime. My first Camino was in the springtime (April-May). There was still snow on the ground atop the Pyrenees in late April, and late spring snow storms are still quite common at this time of year. The Pilgrims Office in SJPP is quite helpful in letting you know the weather conditions over the Route de Napoleon. Heed this advice seriously and take the *Valcarlos* route (the lower way) should it be necessary. Do not take chances with getting lost or stranded on the mountain top. This will not go well. From *Roncesvalles* to *Pamplona*, I experienced cold, drizzly rain intermittently that required wearing my poncho for long periods of the day. When the rain stopped and the sun came out, it was quite pleasant and the temperatures were mild. Mornings and evenings were almost always chilly and required some outer garment such as a fleece or jacket to stay warm. Best advice, from my perspective, is to think in terms of "layers" so you can remove or add, as necessary. From *Burgos* on, I experienced warm and sunny days for a good part of the time, but we were not without cold wind and rain periodically. In *Galicia* you can count on some rain here and there. As the locals say, "If you don't like the weather, wait an hour!" Best part about springtime is all the green fields, yellow rapeseed, and wild flowers galore. The gently blowing wheat fields on the *Meseta* are glorious!

Fall. My second Camino that started in *Leon* occurred during the month of September. Although we did experience some rain, especially in *Galicia*, the temperatures were quite mild and we walked most of the way in shorts and t-shirts. Gone were the green fields, however, but they were replaced by corn fields and the wheat had been harvested and rolled into large circular bales. There were also plenty of seasonal wild flowers that are quite extraordinary if you take the time to stop and look.

Where Will You Stay While on the Camino?

Make a conscious decision on how you are going to travel while on the Camino.

Random *albergues*. Will it be spontaneous, staying in *albergues* as they have space available? (Keep in mind that municipal, parish, convent/monastery, network and association *albergues* do not take reservations, as a rule. Many private *albergues* will take reservations, however.)

Book your own hotels along the way. Will you book your own hotels along the way by calling ahead to get a reservation each day? Of course, you will need some sort of guide book (e.g. Michelin Guide or Brierley) to know where to call. (Allow an hour or so each day to do this.)

Travel Company. If you choose a Travel Company, you will probably need to make your reservation with this company at least three months in advance of your trip. (This is not the rule in all cases, but be safe and enquire about it ahead of time.)

Book your hotels ahead of time before you go. Another alternative is to book your own rooms ahead of time, before you go, if you know exactly which hotel or guest house you want to stay in. You can try this but be prepared to receive a slew of "no rooms available for the dates you request" replies via the internet. While I don't know for sure, it is my thought that the Travel Companies book large blocks of rooms in the most popular hotels per agreements a long time in advance to ensure that they have availabilities for their customers when planning itineraries. Of course, the hotels like pre-booking by the Travel Companies because they get filled up quickly. Whatever cancellations or non-use of pre-bookings occur can easily be filled by the hotel within a very short time. That being said, on my first Camino in May 2013, there were pilgrims with whom I was travelling that were booking into hotels a day or so ahead of time – the same ones at which I was staying for that matter – so I don't want to say this alternative is impossible. These could have been last-minute cancellations as mentioned above. Please be aware that this is a hit or miss situation, and you should be prepared for working the phone in the evening after you arrive at your destination.

On my second Camino, I booked all of my accommodations ahead of time via *www.booking.com* or directly with the hotel on their website. This was a time-consuming process, but it was well worth it, considering the money I saved compared to the cost of the Travel Company. I did this with confidence because I had stayed at many of these hotels on my first trip and was aware of those at which I did not stay the first time.

Unless you absolutely love uncertainty and want to live on the edge here, I can guarantee that you will not want to be spending your time at the end of a long, tiresome day engaging in the stressful activity of trying to find a booking for the following night. You will covet this end-of-the-day time that will allow you to care for your body, your gear, connect with your loved ones at home, just get settled in, eat dinner and get to bed early for a good night's rest.

Finally, I want to make it clear that there may be many of you who will relish the "adventure" of "letting the Camino provide." If this applies to you, then I applaud you wholeheartedly and wish you a *muy buen Camino*!

How Much Time Do You Have, and What Will Be the Length of Your Camino?

Will you walk the entire Camino or will you just have the time or energy to walk a smaller portion? The length of your trip will most likely be primarily determined by how much time you have available and/or the money you have to spend on the trip. For seniors such as myself, you may have all the time in the world, but are limited by a budget that will impact your available time. Once you get this figured out, everything else will flow from there. Whatever you decide, make sure that your travel schedule allows for sufficient time to adjust to jet lag (if you are coming from afar), and that you at least arrive at your starting point the night before. This is especially critical if you are starting the *Camino Frances* in *St. Jean Pied de Port*. You will want to be well-rested for that first day over the Pyrenees which is a strenuous uphill climb and a hazardous downhill descent over sixteen miles in duration.

Of course, the length of your walk will affect several things in your planning process right off the bat. For instance: if you're planning on a one to two-week walk from *Sarria* to *Santiago*, you will need far less gear, and this may affect your decision on what you can carry with you each day. You may not feel that you need a baggage service to take your bags from hotel to hotel – that you can carry everything yourself. On the other hand, if you are walking the entire Camino, you may feel that you need to take more stuff with you, such as clothing and special personal items that you would not be able to carry on your back for the entire 35-40 days.

You may also feel that for a shorter trip, you will be okay with staying in *albergues* along the way – perhaps with a hotel here and there. Think this through and see what you come up with. Getting this sorted out early will have a dramatic effect on your budget and planning process.

How Will You Get to Your Starting Point?

Where are you going to start your Camino? This is a critical factor to establish up front for obvious reasons. If you are on a limited budget, for example, complicated connections may be more-costly – they usually are from my experience. So this factor may determine where you start. Along the *Camino Frances*, there are several "hubs" which will allow good transportation connections from all over Europe. *Pamplona, Burgos, Logrono, Leon, Astorga and Ponferrada* have good connections to either planes or trains from some of the more major cities in Spain. I ran into people all along the *Camino Frances* who started out in one of these places and walked only a week or two. Others eventually went all the way to *Santiago*. I met one chap who flew from Ireland to *Barcelona*, then caught a bus from there to *Logrono*, where he started his walk. He ended in *Leon*. If you are going from *Sarria* to *Santiago*, you can fly into *Santiago* and get easy transportation to *Sarria* from there. You can also get to *Sarria* from *Madrid* via train and bus. Research this thoroughly before you go so as to take the stress out of your travel. Again, you do not want to arrive at your starting point the day you are planning to walk – oh, please do not do this! Best case scenario is to get there early the day before and enjoy a rest and a peaceful sleep before you start out.

For my first Camino, I flew from *Sacramento*, CA to *Dallas* and from there to *Paris*. I took a bus from *Charles de Gaulle* airport (CDG) to *Montparnasse* where I stayed at an inexpensive hotel for two nights. I had two days of sightseeing in *Paris* before taking a train early the next morning from *Montparnasse* to *Bayonne*. From there I changed trains and wound up in *St Jean* about 4 pm. This gave me time to get settled in my hotel, do some sightseeing of *St Jean*, and enjoy a leisurely dinner by the river before going to sleep. The jet lag was gone, and I was ready to roll. I cannot overstate the importance of planning this phase of your trip carefully. Getting up and walking 16 miles over the mountains is unlike anything else you may have experienced in your travels thus far.

For my second Camino, I flew to *Madrid* from *Sacramento*, via *Dallas*. I arrived at MAD at 8:00 am and took a connector train from the airport to *Chamartin* train station in the city, then a train from there to *Leon* arriving at 2:30 pm that day. I could have easily walked the following day, but I wanted to spend some extra time in *Leon* and show my wife the sights there.

Madrid is certainly a good arrival point, no matter from where you are starting your Camino, due to the many connections that are available to almost any place along the *Camino Frances* or *Camino Portugues*. As I mentioned earlier, I have heard about many pilgrims who took trains or busses to *Pamplona* and made their way from there to either *Roncesvalles* or SJPP via shared cabs, bus or private drivers.

Remove the travel stress, and you will be all the better off. It is well worth the cost of a couple of extra days -- on the front end especially. At the end, you may want to get home as quickly as possible, but there is wisdom in winding down an extra day in *Santiago*, not to mention saving a couple of extra days to perhaps take a trip to *Muxia* or *Finesterre*.

↓ travel stress

Chapter Three

Preparation

This chapter is all about preparing yourself **physically, mentally, and spiritually** for your wonderful walk in Spain. I feel compelled to add a word or two here as a way of being inclusive, as well as cautionary. There are many who will say that all you really need to go on the Camino are three things basically: (1) your willingness to go, (2) a complete surrender of your stubbornness and negative thought processes, and (3) an understanding "deep within" that "the Camino will provide." I must say that there is a certain amount of freedom in this approach, a complete abandonment and randomness that has great appeal to the adventurous ones out there. I do admire this spirit, and if this describes you and your outlook, then please skip this chapter, or the whole book for that matter. *Ultreia y Buen Camino*!

If, however, you are like many of us who have to scrape together the funds over an extended period of time to pay for the trip, you may want to put in the time and effort to adequately prepare physically for the experience and not be forced to drop out and go home due to an injury or medical condition that might have possibly been avoided. Also, had you not been prepared mentally and spiritually as well, you might find yourself discouraged for some reason, or disappointed after walking for several days because the experience did not live up to your "expectations." I have encountered more than a few pilgrims who were facing these issues somewhere along the 500 miles. Some were able to overcome whatever it was with the help of others, and some dropped out and went home, sadly, and had nothing good to say about the experience, I imagine.

What follows in the next pages then is some advice, based on my own experience of course and, where applicable, some helpful "notes" that may add to your knowledge as you prepare for your own trip. I offer the following disclaimers. Please keep in mind that I have no experience as a professional trainer or medic nor am I a licensed counselor by any stretch of the imagination. I am just a fellow pilgrim, like you, with some good experience under my belt.

Physical Preparation

Two and one half years before my first trip, I had back surgery to remove and repair a broken disc in my lower vertebrae. A piece of the disc between L4 and L5 had broken off and was lodged in the spinal column, causing severe sciatic nerve pain and partial paralysis of my right leg and foot. I was literally quite crippled by this injury and unable to walk normally without assistance from a cane. Often, without any warning, my right leg would collapse, and I would fall on the spot. At the time this injury occurred, I had gone back to work after having been retired for two years. I was working as a lending officer at a bank, which required that I be sitting at my desk in front of a computer for hours at a time. This sedentary situation was tormenting for me and had a dramatic impact on my effectiveness at my job. I was in pain all through the day and night, unable to sleep well, if at all, and the pain medication was beginning to take its toll on my thought processes. Finally, the health insurance bureaucracy allowed for a MRI, and the spine surgeons scheduled my surgery immediately after discovering what was really wrong. After the operation, it was 30 days, recovering at home, before I could even go back to work. But it soon became apparent that a return to sitting at a desk was just not in the cards for me, so I retired once again, this time for good. Slowly, I began to respond to the post-op physical therapy and was able to regain strength in my leg and back. I never did fully regain the feeling in my right leg, and to this day, a significant portion of my leg is still numb. The doctors told me that at my age, this could quite possible be the best I could hope for. Eventually, I began to realize that I needed to practice what was really "mind over matter." I knew that my leg would work, but I just couldn't feel it. This literally meant that I had to step out in faith. It took quite a lot of getting used to it, I will say. I owe a lot of my recovery during this period to my wife, Heather, who encouraged me to get out and start walking again. She would accompany me on the walks and watch me from behind to see how I was walking, correcting me when I began to favor the "bad" leg. This kept me from developing bad habits, and without doubt speeded up the rehabilitation period. Before long, perhaps six months, I was able to walk "normally" once again, so once I decided to go to on this crazy adventure, it was just a matter of getting in shape.

Long before leaving for both Caminos, I spent months preparing for the trip by training to walk long distances. I logged many hours on trails around and about the American River and Lake Natomas in the Fair Oaks, Orangevale and Folsom, California area. This was an attempt on my part to simulate what I expected to encounter along the *Camino Frances*. As it turned out, I was both right and wrong about some of my assumptions. While I subsequently found that I was prepared to walk long distances, I discovered at the same time that I was not fully trained for the many "ups and downs" that I actually encountered.

On the first Camino, my friend Greg was able to handle the strenuous uphill portions much greater than I, but found himself struggling with the downhill parts. I was the opposite. For some reason, the downs were easier for me. The result of this was that, although we walked at different paces going up, I was usually able to "catch up" on the down. By the time we arrived in Pamplona, we were both suffering from calf muscle pain that made it very painful to go down stairs in the hotel. My wife Heather suggested via email that we try "rolling" our calf muscles if possible. We heeded this advice and "rolled" our muscles by sitting near the edge of the bed in the hotel and moving our calves up and down on the edge. That definitely helped, and within a day or so, we were able to walk it out, and we were not bothered by it again. I now know that there are "techniques" of walking up and down hills that will greatly alleviate or prevent pain and injury.

NOTE: On challenging uphill or downhill tracks, practice taking small steps forward without too much lateral movement. This will take longer, but you will benefit from this technique on the big hills in Spain.

Preparing for the second Camino, Heather and I walked literally hundreds of miles over a six-month training period with backpacks weighted to approximate what we expected to carry in Spain, but we did not put the needed time into building up our "quad" muscles sufficiently. This mistake resulted in a quad injury for Heather that severely hampered her walk on several occasions.

NOTE: Ask your trainer, or research the appropriate "squat" exercises for you so you can build up strength and avoid these problems. Find steep hills to climb up and down as part of your regular training regimen. If you have no hills where you live, perhaps there is a nearby stadium at a high-school/college or an office building that will allow you climb up and down the steps there. Maybe you have a stair master in your gym or health club. Any of these will help get you ready for the hills that you will most certainly encounter.

By far, the biggest issue that faces most of us is preventing, or learning how to cope with, the dreaded blisters. Almost everyone gets blisters on their feet at some point along the Camino. This can turn out to be a minor irritation or a major problem. Do not minimize the vast importance of blister prevention and treatment *before* leaving. On my first Camino blisters turned out to be a major story and almost caused me to drop out! If you are training sufficiently before you go, you will most likely see where blisters may affect you. Read up on blister prevention from different sources and then choose what best suits you based on your personal experience. Prevention ranges from proper shoe or boot fit to determining whether or not to use liner socks to techniques of applying salves or powders of all sorts directly to your feet. This may require plenty of experimentation on your part, but this effort will turn out to be the best thing you can do to get ready. Take my word for it.

NOTE: It is my opinion that spending time and money on getting the right fit on your shoes or boots, choosing the right socks for your feet in those boots, and logging the training miles to see how it works out will be the single most important thing you do to get ready. It sounds simple, but if you can't walk on your feet because of the pain of blisters, you're done! Be ready, do what you need to do, and have the right first aid should you need it. Remember, that there are pharmacies (Farmacias) all over the Camino wherein you can find all you need to treat your "Ampollas."

You will no doubt hear, read or see many blister stories from various sources, whether they be travel guides or YouTube videos, or perhaps anecdotes that are spun by word of mouth as you travel along. All of them contain remedies and things that you "absolutely" must do to treat blisters. You will have to determine what is right for your unique situation.

Options for treatment are widespread on the Camino, since *Ampollas* are such a common injury. At many *albergues* along the way, there are "blister gurus" who have become legendary, so to speak. They spend hours every day treating pilgrims as they come through. Medical Clinics (*Centros Salud*) are available in most towns. They are certainly well-equipped, and they will treat you, should that be necessary.

So, here is my blister story: On my first Camino, I got all the way to *Logrono* without any major foot problems, just some minor irritation on a couple of toes on which I put band-aids. (BTW: This had happened to me on my training walks, so I was ready for that.) In *Logrono*, I went out to dinner at night in my *Teva* sandals and, not paying close attention, I carelessly tripped on a stone curb, severely stubbing my right big toe. I went down hard on the stone walkway, much to the dismay of two Spanish girls who were sitting at a nearby table enjoying a glass of wine. I can still see the look of horror on their faces as they saw me there splattered out at their feet. When I was able to get up, I determined that there were no other injuries that I could tell and I stumbled inside to the restaurant and sat at a table to order dinner. During the meal, the toe began to throb mercilessly, and I was in excruciating pain. After the meal, and limping back to the hotel with my friend's assistance, I determined that the toe must have been broken. Fear crept into my brain, and I could see the very real possibility that I would not be able to finish my Camino. I tried putting my boots on, and that effort was successful. The toe hurt badly, but I was able to put my full weight down on the foot. My friend Greg insisted that I could not walk the next day since we were scheduled to go 18 miles to *Najera*. I decided that I would take 800mg of Ibuprofen and get some sleep and see how things turned out in the morning. When I woke up, the throbbing had stopped but I was still able to put weight on the foot as long as it was inside the boot. I experimented with a gait that would enable me to walk with a short step, but after careful consideration, I determined that it would be best to take a bus to *Najera* and give the foot at least another day of rest. In the morning, Greg took off to walk and I took a cab to the bus station and got a ticket for *Najera*. There was plenty of room on the bus which meant that I could find an empty seat next to me to put my leg up. By 10:00 am, I was in *Najera* and limped the short distance from the bus stop to my hotel. The more I walked the more encouraged I became. Perhaps my toe was not broken after all but merely badly tweaked. I rested the foot for most of the remainder of the day, forgoing any sightseeing, and then enjoyed a good dinner.

In the morning, I decided to try walking, using the gait that I had developed earlier. The walk to *Santo Domingo* was 13 miles, and the weather was good and mostly mild that day so there were no issues with moisture seeping in. By the time I arrived, I was tired, and the toe hurt but was none the worse for wear. I continued walking like this for the next few days, considering myself to be quite clever. By the time I arrived in *Carrion de los Condes*, I felt as if I had dodged a bullet with the toe, and was more inclined to think that I just experienced a really bad stubbing. That evening, we set out to town from our hotel on the outskirts to find a place that might be open to eat an early dinner. I put on my running shoes, as I usually did in the evening (no more sandals walking in the city!) and set out. We could not find any restaurants open and decided to head back to the hotel and eat there later. On the way, I could feel that my left heel was quite sore and irritated. When I got back to the room and took off my shoes, I discovered that I had a huge blister on that heel! There was already fluid in the blister, so I put some protective gauze bandage on it and covered it with tape. That evening I walked gingerly about and prayed that the blister would go down by the morning. It did not. While I could fit into my boot OK, I found I would have to readjust my gait to favor that heel. This resulted in eventually developing a blister on the right heel by the time I arrived in *Sahagun*. Now I had two large blisters.

It was in *Sahagun* that I met a guy from Seattle who was a self-professed "expert" on blisters. He was a pleasant fellow, but was insisting that I had to puncture and drain the blisters and stay off them for a day or so. This treatment was one I had heard about from other pilgrims, but I could not stay off my feet for a couple of days since I had hotel reservations and it just wasn't an option for me. I went into a *Farmacia* next to my hotel and got some supplies from the pharmacist and went about the painstaking process of bandaging and treating for possible infection.

Although I walked in pain a good portion of the time, I made it to *Santiago*. While there, the original blister had broken and was drained and beginning to heal. The other was still active. My bandaging technique worked but it took me about one hour each day after my shower at the end of the day to get it right. As it turned out, the blisters didn't prevent me from finishing my Camino, but they certainly hampered it.

For my second Camino with Heather, I had purchased new Keen boots that were ¾ length, not low cuts. Over six months, they were well broken in. The boots fit me beautifully, I used only one pair of wool socks, and I walked 17 days in Spain with not one blister. Heather was another story. She had blisters all over both feet, but she bandaged up with *Compeed* and tape before they became fluid-filled, and she made it. It is important to point out that Heather experienced the same type of blisters on her training walks before going, so she was prepared to deal with them in Spain.

Mental Preparation

Another aspect of getting ready is to prepare yourself mentally for going on a long pilgrimage. By this, I mean coming to terms about your reasons for making this trip. If at all possible, try not to leave any "unfinished business" behind that might cloud your mind, occupy your thoughts, and preclude your ability to "enjoy the moment." Undoubtedly you will have family or friends who will subtly, or perhaps even blatantly, question your sanity for wanting to walk 500 miles across a country in Europe. I remember Heather telling me that before she walked, an acquaintance had asked her, "What is your real motive for doing this?" As she described it to me, the question stopped her short in her tracks, and she was left without an answer. The question appeared to be fraught with hidden meaning and some unspoken resentment or jealousy.

Of course, I don't think that we are under any obligation whatsoever to justify our decision to walk the Camino, but you may find resistance from those closest to you upon whose support you may be counting. Just know that this unexpected reaction may happen when you announce what you're planning to do. Many younger pilgrims find resistance from parents concerned about their safety, whereas older pilgrims often find resistance from adult children concerned about health issues that could occur. These are not unreasonable concerns, but you can address them in a calm and rational way if you have prepared to do so. The support of our loved ones is important to all of us. The sharing of your plans to them should be positioned in such a way as to allay some, if not all, of the fears that they might have for your safety or health.

If you put no thought into this part of your preparation, you may fuel the fire unnecessarily and cause conflict that need not be there. In this regard, it is important to note that I am certainly aware that not all situations are identical, to say the least. Even the most-calm and rational approach may eventually fall on deaf ears. But at least you will have demonstrated your personal preparation and be able to leave on your journey with a clear conscience, so to speak.

Most of the fears of our loved ones revolve around the issue of us being "out of touch" with them. So, make a plan that will allay this fear by establishing ahead of time a method of communication that will work for your individual situation. As an example: if you are planning to take a smart phone with you, you will be able to obtain internet connection through Wi-Fi just about anywhere. On my first Camino, and with only two exceptions, I emailed my wife every night to let her know I was safe. Additionally, I posted pictures and some brief comments on Facebook every day to keep all my friends and family up-to-date. This process took me about 20 to 30 minutes every day, but I disciplined myself to do it as soon as I got settled into where I was staying for the night. I can't tell you how many comments I had from so many people who felt as if they were travelling along with me. It was very encouraging to me, and it kept my heart light and my mind free to accomplish what I had to do and to enjoy every moment. A woman from Australia who walked a good part of the way with us had an international plan on her iPhone. When she got into a town we were all staying at, the first thing she did was call her mother who was ill to check on her. She shared with us that this took a great load off her mind.

Explain to your loved ones that you have a plan in this regard. Tell them what you will do on a regular basis, and take control of the situation. If your smart phone works as a telephone overseas, set it up so that it is turned off unless you want it to work as a phone. I think I can safely say that you will most likely not want it to be ringing at all times while you are walking. Some people were using Skype, WhatsApp, or some other application to communicate with their families. It is all a matter of personal preference. Discover what will work for you and tell your loved ones what they can expect.

Spiritual Preparation

The Camino de Santiago is the oldest Christian pilgrimage in existence. Its beginnings can be traced back to the 9th century, and you will find that Christian spirituality surrounds you everywhere as you make your way from the many starting points in Europe to the city of St. James. James and his brother John were the sons of Zebedee and two of the first disciples called by Jesus. Truthfully, not much is known of James' presence in Iberia during the 1st century, but this has not stopped the Spanish people in their reverence of the man who became their patron saint, and who later achieved legendary proportions, becoming known as *Santiago Matamoros*, the Vanquisher of the Moors when the Muslims had conquered all of Spain. In spite of all this rich historical background, there are tens of thousands of pilgrims who are walking the Camino every year with absolutely no knowledge of these things and without any spiritual intent whatsoever. They walk for personal reasons that have nothing to do with any religious fervor or purpose. Some walk for the physical challenge and others for social reasons, and still others to experience the sheer beauty of the surroundings and to immerse themselves in Spanish culture, festivals and food. You may choose to disregard all of the art and architecture that flowed from this vast religious experience through the ages, but you would be missing a large part of the culture and the history of Spain.

As you walk, you will find that most conversations will eventually come around to the question of why you are walking the Camino. On my first Camino, I was surprised at how many people I encountered who were intrigued about walking the Camino as a result of seeing the movie, *The Way*. When this motivation was uncovered, it moved the conversation along the lines of "how did you get from seeing that movie to being here?" I talked with many pilgrims who, as it turned out, considered themselves to be religious or spiritual people, but for some reason did not give that as a reason for their walk. They expressed that it was just a challenge, had been on their "bucket list," or just thought it would be a cool thing to do. As the miles piled up however, and the troubles hit (i.e. blisters, injuries, illness, rain, mud), they began to rely on prayer and the prayers of those back home to get them through, as well as all the immediate help they received from their fellow pilgrims and *hospitaleros* along the way.

My personal spirituality is rooted in my devotion to Jesus Christ as my Lord and Savior as you could tell from my comments in the Introduction to this book. I try to follow Him all the days of my life. This is what guides me every day in every way. This spiritual formation in the Kingdom of God informs all that I do and how I relate to all those around me, and I try, not always successfully, to be salt and light in this dark world.

On a desolate dirt road in the black forest of *Montes de Oca*, I found myself alone, physically hurting, and afraid. All I could think to do was pray the Jesus Prayer: "Lord Jesus Christ, Son of God, have mercy on me, a sinner." I repeated the prayer over and over. After a few moments, I noticed that my pace had picked up quite appreciatively, and I was no longer feeling any pain.

The reason for spiritual preparation before you go is simply to point out that you will undoubtedly experience intense events that may cause you to come to the end of your rope, moments which may ultimately cause you to question not only your reason or purpose in taking this trip, but will throw you into a tailspin of doubt and depression. Ask yourself the important questions before you go. What is my source of strength? Where do you go when all else fails? What are my expectations? I have seen many pilgrims in deep despair because of disappointments and unrealistic expectations – not to mention the added impact of physical injuries.

Maybe the most important question is: What are my expectations? A wise person once said that "expectations are just planned resentments." I have a couple of examples. I ran into a woman in a *hostel* in *Rabanal* who apparently had a whole bunch of unrealistic expectations that I surmised were based on previous experiences that she most likely had from staying in luxurious vacation spots in the world. Whatever the case might be, these expectations were simply not part of the Camino experience common to us all. This was most likely her first night on the Camino and she was complaining about everything because it was not up to what she thought it should be. Another young man I know of dropped out and sadly went home after two weeks because he did not meet anyone with a similar lifestyle along the way, and he was lonely. Both of these individuals expressed anger and resentment at the circumstances in front of them. I am certain that to this day they would not speak favorably of the Camino because of these experiences. You may say that these are just personality issues, but I would submit to you that there are unfulfilled expectations here that have a lot to do with the spiritual condition of the individual.

When Heather and I returned from our 2015 trip, we were invited to do a presentation at our church about our trip. At one point during the presentation, the pastor asked us what spiritual lessons we had learned. Heather spoke of her personal growth, her appreciation of me being by her side all the way, and the deep blessing of carrying the prayers of the congregation to the foot of the *Cruz de Ferro*. When it was my turn, I could only think that I would say the same things. What came out was "ditto", but also the simple statement that each day on the Camino we get up, walk out the front door, turn to the west and put one foot in front of the other until we get to our destination for the night. Along the way we fully enjoy everything we encounter. Then we get up and do it again, and again, and again. We should all contemplate that routine as a daily way of life.

Wherever your spirituality is rooted is your business alone. Do yourself a favor, however, and look in the mirror before you go on any adventure and deal with it. Of course, this is true with life in general, but we pilgrims have come to understand that the *Camino* is certainly both a microcosm of life as well as a metaphor for living. Know that your whole value system may be called into question, and you may come to the end of yourself real fast while walking in the middle of nowhere in a driving rain storm, climbing a difficult mountain, or lost in a black forest. It happened to me in that olive orchard in Mexico, and it happened again in the *Montes de Oca* between *Belorado* and *San Juan*.

NOTE: *What follows next is a day to day journey along the Camino Frances based on my personal experiences in May 2013 and September 2015. This is a little bit of travelogue and a little bit of guide book with some cultural or historical highlights thrown in every so often. I hope you enjoy hearing about my adventures.*

Buen Camino!

Chapter Four

Traveling to St. Jean Pied de Port

April 23, 2013 – Paris, France. The SCNF train to *Bayonne* was scheduled to leave *Montparnasse* Station at 7:28 am, so we were up early and walked the three blocks to the station to arrive an hour ahead of time. There was a large board that hung in the center of the station indicating the destinations and gates, but we could see no *Bayonne* train as yet. I found the information booth and asked there about our train, and was told that it was still too early for it to be posted. We were just to wait and eventually it would come up showing the proper gate.

At 7:20, the menu finally clicked over to show the *Bayonne* train at Gate 6 and suddenly there was a mad rush from the main concourse. We followed the cattle call and found that we were near the back of the pack by this point. Now we couldn't figure what coach to get on. A nearby gentleman, who noticed our confusion, offered to help get us on the right car. Eventually we boarded the correct coach and found our seats after stowing our bags away on top. It was a very comfortable and spacious coach with adjustable seats, and soon we were settled in for the 5-hour trip. We pulled out of *Montparnasse* on time and were outside the city in less than half an hour. After a while, we found that we were getting hungry and took turns going to the dining car to get some food. Greg went first and came back with water and some fruit. I made my trip and found some fresh-brewed coffee and pastries which I brought back to the seat. This was turning out to be a delightful trip so far until we discovered that we had a problem adult child directly in front of us. As the sun began to come in our shared window, he closed the blinds, apparently because his laptop screen was hard to see. This meant that we could not see out to view the countryside. Greg pulled the shade open and the guy abruptly closed it again. This was getting annoying, and Greg smiled at me and re-opened the blinds. Now the guy was getting ticked off and stood up and muttered some cuss words in French at us while violently closing the blinds. He was a young 30-something who was dressed in warm ups and looked as if he had spent many hours in the gym. There was no conductor in sight to arbitrate this matter, and since neither Greg nor I were going to challenge him to a fight, we thought it best to try and change our seats. Fortunately, there were two seats in the same car down a few rows and we got up and moved. Now we had a window all our own, and hopefully no one would get on at a subsequent stop to claim them. We kept the seats the rest of the way and made it to *Bayonne* on time. When we got off the train, we found that we had approximately two hours to wait to make the connection to *St Jean Pied de Port*, so we got our luggage and trudged through the small, quaint station to the outside area where we found a table outside a cafe. A waitress soon arrived and we ordered some food. Greg ordered a grilled sandwich and fries and I got a tuna sandwich and a beer. She brought a full array of condiments, including mustard. This would be the last time we would see a container of mustard for nearly 40 days!

Just behind Greg, I could see our bully from the train leaving the station and moving out into the town proper. I think we were both somewhat relieved that he would not be going on any further. When the time arrived, we got our gear together and headed upstairs on the other side of the station to the platform from where our connecting train was leaving. Soon there was a rush of many pilgrims attempting to do the same thing with fingers being pointed in many directions. We boarded what appeared to be the right train and found that there were about fifty others that shared that opinion. Stowing our bags in the compartments above, we found a seat. The car was packed with pilgrims, many standing with just a backpack and walking sticks.

The ride to *St Jean Pied de Port* lasted about 1 1/2 hours and was relatively uneventful. The passengers were generally quite gregarious and talkative, and we began to feel the *camaraderie* that we would experience again and again on our adventure. Although I could not tell for sure, it appeared that we were the only Americans on that train except for one woman, whom we would later encounter on a few occasions. It was interesting sitting there and listening to the various conversations around me, trying to figure out what they were saying. We were both in a great mood and feeling quite rested at this point.

Our small train made several stops along the way at tiny, quaint towns in the *Basque* provinces on the eastern slopes of the Pyrenees. Along the way, the topography seemed almost jungle-like at times with very dense vines and thick forests, then cleared out when we got to a stop. We arrived on time in *St Jean* at about 4 pm, got our bags down and began the walk from the station to the *Hotel Central*. The afternoon sun was beginning to settle over the mountains in the distance, but the town was still bathed in beautiful shadows. This is really a picturesque village with so much to see. It really deserves a longer stay if one has the opportunity. After a short walk from the train station, we arrived at the *Hotel Central* right in the middle of town and checked in. Madame Cheret greeted us warmly at the front desk and our bags were carried upstairs to the room by a friendly fellow who thought we were Irish because of my hat (from the Shamrock Half Marathon in Sacramento). Greg remarked at the man's strength carrying both bags, and he proudly displayed his arm muscles, indicating that it was "*Basque strength*"! The room was huge compared to our room in Paris. There were windows overlooking the river *Nive* in the bedroom area as well as the bathroom. While Greg got in the bath for clean up first, I went downstairs and got the Wi-Fi connection straightened out with a special code. Somewhat complicated, but nothing like the code for the Paris Hotel. Madame Cheret said that dinner would be served at 7:30 in the dining room and that breakfast would be at 8am the next morning. She showed me where to leave the bags in the morning so they could be picked up by the bag service. I returned to the room to find that Greg had finished in the bath and I instructed him on the Wi-Fi, which did not seem to work for his iPhone. This was the first of many instances where one code was necessary for each phone. I got my bath and took some video of the river below us. Greg and I then set out to walk around the town. We walked through the arch along *Rue L'Eglise* and turned left on *Rue d'Espagne* which turned into *Rue de Citadelle*. At the top of the street we could see the steep path heading upwards toward the *Citadelle* and decided to check it out. There were phenomenal views from this high perch above the town, and we gazed across the city towards the mountains which we were about to scale tomorrow.

As we headed back down *Rue de Citadelle*, we noticed many pilgrims lining up outside some of the *albergues*, trying to get a bed for the night. Although I had known this before the trip started, I was now beginning to see first-hand the issues of life in the *albergues*. Most of us had arrived on the same train from *Paris*, but many had not yet found a place to stay – and here we were having already checked in and cleaned up for the evening. This was a scene that would repeat itself over and over again in the six weeks to come.

There is an adventurous, spontaneous piece that is missing when one stays in a reserved hotel room, and certainly a dramatic difference in cost, but there is also that comfort in knowing that there is a room and a private hot shower or bath waiting, no matter what time you get in. Neither Greg nor I were ever sorry we had made the choice to book our hotels ahead of time. We were able to sleep soundly, and we were always well-rested for the next day.

Back down in the town, we decided to find some food for our trip the next day. There was a small market that had fruit and cheese and bread, but it was already closed for the day. We felt that we could supplement whatever we needed from the breakfast in the morning. We also found an outfitting store that sold trekking gear and Camino paraphernalia. I considered buying one of the hats, but decided to save the money for something I really wanted or needed later on. We looked at several of the restaurants that were surrounding the main downtown area, and discovered that they were not yet serving dinner, but just snacks and drinks. Some very nice outdoor cafes in this area. We decided to go back to the hotel and eat in the restaurant there. After heading back to the room, we were able to get Greg hooked up on Wi-Fi, and he contacted Marianne, his wife, on Facebook. I did the same and posted some pictures of the view from our room as well as a really bucolic photo of the River *Nive*.

Dinner was elegant, and one of the nicest we were to have on the entire trip. We had the local red wine that was bottled in town. I had a cheese omelet and Greg had a serving of salmon. Delicious. Soon after dinner we headed back to the room and hit the sack.

Chapter Five
St. Jean Pied de Port to Pamplona

Day One, SJPP to Roncesvalles

Greg had set an alarm on his iPhone to get us up on time. We both slept very well. We got our main bags packed and lugged them downstairs to the proscribed area. Madame Cheret surprised us by already having breakfast ready earlier than expected. We had orange juice, toast, butter, eggs, croissants, and strawberry jam. I had a large pot of coffee all to myself — something I did not know would be a rare occurrence in the days to come. There were some oranges and apples that we took with us for our backpacks to include in our provisions for lunch. At this point, Greg and I were primarily concerned about the weather conditions for our trek over the mountain. We had agreed that if the weather was bad, we would not take the *Route Napoleon*, but would opt for the lower route that was longer but not as dangerous in rain and snow. Madame Cheret cheerfully informed us that the weather report was for clear skies today, so we should encounter no difficulties, but that would not be the case for the next few days when heavy rain was forecast. So, thinking that our timing was good, we decided to give it a go. We were able to leave the hotel by 8:30am, stop at the market on the way to obtain the bread and cheese, and it was just a short walk until we were at the outskirts of St. Jean and headed up the road that led to the way over the mountain. There was a continual grade uphill for at least four miles as we wandered through countryside that was in full springtime bloom. Before long, we decided to strip down to t-shirts and shorts, because the temperature was getting to what appeared to be about 80 degrees F.

Greg was moving on ahead of me, his pace being much faster going up the hill. We agreed that he should keep going and I would catch up later. Just beyond *Huntto*, the trail veered off to the left and up a steep rocky hill. About 1 kilometer up the trail from here, I came across two people who were stopped to take a rest. I stopped also and we began to chat. The man, Charlie, was from Liverpool, England and the woman was American. They were not together, but had just met up on the trail. As we started to walk together, I found out that Charlie had been on the Camino about two years earlier, but did not finish because his feet bothered him so badly. He said that he had gotten as far as *Sarria* and had to drop out. The woman was called Claire, and she was from Pleasanton, CA, and I remembered seeing her on the train from *Bayonne*. Claire explained that she was between jobs at home and was determined to make the trip all by herself. She stated that her husband was dithering about preparing to go, so she just decided to stop waiting for him, not knowing when she would have another opportunity to go.

At one point, I made a statement that if we could all just get through today, the worst part of the trip was over. When Charlie heard this, he threw his head back and laughed uproariously, "That would definitely *not* be the case, mate!" And then he laughed for a while. When I asked him to clarify, he said that there were many challenges ahead, some of them quite daunting.

By now, Claire was really struggling to get up the mountain. Charlie was trying as best he could to council her on walking and what she needed to do to make it. It was clear to all who saw her that she was not prepared for the trip and the physical rigors the walk demanded. She told me she walked around the Oakland hills all the time, but her physical condition belied this. Claire still felt she could make it even though, at this point, she was only one-third of the way to *Roncesvalles*. At the pace she was moving, it was unlikely that she could make sufficient headway to avoid darkness in the woods on the other side of the mountains. We tried to convince her to stop at *Orisson* and get a taxi back to *St. Jean*. From there she could take a bus to *Roncesvalles*, and then go on. As we approached *Orisson*, she appeared to be considering this. Greg and I kept on going at *Orisson*, and we didn't see her the rest of the day. It appeared that Charlie stopped at *Orisson*, too, and we did not see him for the rest of the day, or the rest of the trip, for that matter. It occurred to me that he might have taken transportation to *Sarria*, and then finished the trip from there.

That day, going up, there were many other fellow pilgrims we kept encountering. We would pass them, then they would pass us, and so on and so forth. Of particular interest was a trio of guys who were traveling with very light packs. They were middle-aged and were moving along at a rapid pace up the hill. Even Greg had a hard time keeping up with them, and after a couple of kilometers, they left him in the dust. We saw these guys many days later on and had some interesting discussions with one of them.

Near the top, we were privileged to encounter a large flock of Griffon Vultures (about 2 dozen). These are magnificent creatures with wingspans of 8 feet. We watched them circle around a distant valley, perhaps waiting for some sheep to die. In many respects, they reminded me of the California Condors.

After about 8 hours, we thought we had reached *Col. Lepoeder*, but a passing Brit warned us that we still had some "ups" to go. It was about one mile later that we began the final ascent. By this time, there was snow still remaining on the ground, and the wind increased its ferocity. I kept telling myself to take "one step at a time" and I would somehow make it to the top. Looking up the trail and then down, there was no one in sight. I needed to take a leak, so I just stopped by a tree at the side of the road and did my business. I noticed that my urine was a very dark color, accentuated by the snow. This was a sure sign of de-hydration, so I made it a point to force water on myself to avoid any further complications. Finally, *Col. Lepoeder* was in front of me, and just around a rock sat Greg smiling and waiting for me to catch up. Soon we began the long and extremely steep climb down. The first 50 meters or so was deep snow, and I found that the easiest way to navigate my way down was to ski it. I put the poles in the ground and slid down with my boots performing quite well as skis. From there it was dense woods all around, with calf-deep leaves sometimes and then long stretches of rock and root-strewn paths.

After 11 hours we finally reached *Roncesvalles*, and turned right at the side of the *La Posada* hostel and up the short incline to *Casa Beneficiado*, our hotel for the night. This is a remarkable place with stone floors throughout and all recently remodeled. Our room had a separate living area with sofa and arm chairs, a full kitchen, and a very modern bathroom with a glorious shower. We were too late to make the early dinner at 7:30, so we had to opt for the later one at 8:30. The hosts conducted us to a large table that we shared with approximately 12 people. Closest to us was a middle-aged French couple and a young woman from New Zealand. Across the table were some pleasant French folks who were actually eager to show off their English speaking abilities. The older French couple spoke no English, so it was time to test my ability to remember my French. Surprisingly, it came back to me quicker than I thought it would. Altogether it was quite a cordial experience for our first night on The Camino. For the meal, I had a delicious vegetable soup and grilled pork with French fries. Wine and dessert were included. The Wi-Fi connection only worked in the lobby, so Greg and I spent some time sitting there in comfortable arm chairs connecting with home and sending some pictures via Facebook. It was all we could do to stay awake, and soon we were fast asleep in our comfortable room.

Day Two, Roncesvalles to Zubiri

We had a good sleep in *Roncesvalles* at *Casa Beneficiado*. After a very good breakfast, we grabbed some fruit from the buffet, packed everything up and set out. The streets were wet, so it appeared that it had rained the night before. For now, we could see that the rain had stopped. Just down the road was the iconic sign that indicated 790 kilometers to Santiago. The French couple, who were last night's dinner companions, caught up to us and offered to take our picture together next to the road sign.

Within the first five minutes, the rain started coming down, so we had to stop and get our ponchos on. *Burguete* was the first of several charming Basque towns that we passed through. At the town outskirts we met an elderly German couple, Hermann and Gerta, from *Dusseldorf*. Further on into *Burguete*, we were suddenly stopped by a local resident who let us know that we had missed the turn-off for the Camino, while pointing to where we should have gone. This was quite helpful, since we would have most likely gone a long way before we realized it.

Greg fell down in *Burguete* when he tripped over a curb, but he escaped any serious injury. After a while we had to stop for Greg to fix the liner in his right boot that was rubbing against his toe causing some discomfort. We found a shelter out of the rain that had comfortable benches that was quite suitable for fixing stuff and getting a morning snack.

The rain continued as we climbed out of town and now it was getting quite cold. My hands were raw and red by this time, and I had to stop and search my pack for gloves that I had brought, but discovered that I had left them in my luggage. It was then that I devised a method of walking by carrying both of my trekking poles in one hand and shoving the other hand in my pocket. Then I would switch it and go the other way when the first hand warmed up.

By the time we got to *Espinal,* we were both hungry and found a bar in the middle of town that seemed to be popular with other pilgrims and decided to stop there. The rain had momentarily let up, so we took off our backpacks and left them outside and covered them with our ponchos. While doing this, we met an American family of 4 from St. Louis who started the Camino in *Roncesvalles* due to inclement weather reports over the Pyrenees. They recommended the homemade sausage sandwiches being served in the bar, and this sounded good to us. We went inside and ordered our first *"bocadilla"*, but were not impressed.

The bar did allow us to fill our water bottles, so we did that and set out on our way. Again the rain started up and we moved through *Viskaret*. Then we climbed up some slippery trails to a beautiful forest overlooking our destination for the night: *Zubiri*.

At the ancient bridge that guards the little town and crosses the *rio Arga*, we met up again with the fellow from St. Louis who was in the process of booking a room for his family at the *Etxea Hotel* right by the bridge. We said goodbye and headed into town further and found our resting spot, The *Zubiri Hotel*. It did not look like much from the outside, but the interior was very pleasant and the rooms were small but clean and comfortable. The host in the hotel was very cordial and could speak English quite well. Dinner was at 8pm, and we really looked forward to it after a long wet day. At dinner, the same French couple from the night before was at the next table, and we continued our "conversation" as well as we could. The Wi-Fi worked well in the room, and we were able to communicate with home.

Day Three, Zubiri to Pamplona

Another great breakfast from our congenial host with some fruit to spare for the trip. Stepping outside we could see that the rain was still coming down hard, so we had to gear up with the ponchos, which were barely dry from yesterday. When we got to *Larrasoana*, we decided to keep moving instead of crossing the old bridge and seeing the town because the rain was so hard. We then climbed a steep paved path that led up to the little village of *Akaretta*. When we arrived there, the rain stopped and the sun came out. In *Akaretta* is the *casa rural* that was in the movie *The Way*, the place where Tom met the woman from Canada. We took our ponchos off and then set out for *Zuriain*, where we stopped for lunch at yet another old bridge where I was able to get down most of my apple before the rain picked up again.

At the outskirts of this town, we had to follow the busy N135 for awhile and then we veered off the road and up to *Irotz*. Past *Irotz*, we climbed to a very narrow path through dense woods that was muddy and quite slippery. To our amazement, there were several mountain bikers on this trail also. They appeared to be a group of Italians who were having a loud adventure! Their presence made this part of the walk extremely hazardous due to the muddy conditions and narrowness of the trail. The bikers were not experienced riders, we also noted, because they didn't really know what they were doing. And that also added to the danger. Finally, the bikers were gone, and after a few miles the sun peaked through just as we arrived at a rest area near *Zabaldika*. It felt good to sit down and grab a snack. Greg peeled an orange and we split it.

While we were resting, a woman whom we had encountered several times, caught up to us and we chatted with her for awhile. She turned out to be American, from Alaska. She told us of a companion that was walking along with her and with whom she had lost contact. After she gave us a description, we told her that we had seen the woman in *Zuriain*, and she appeared to be limping quite a lot. Before long, the Alaskan woman took off up the hill and we followed about five minutes later. Once again, the hill was quite steep and Greg got way ahead of me. The trail became quite isolated. Before long, nature called, and I really had to stop. I found a secluded spot, and it turned out well with all the stuff I was carrying in my pack (TP, hand sanitizer, wipes, etc.) This was the first "outdoor occasion" of the trip, so I was wondering how it might work out.

After another half hour or so, I met up with Greg who was waiting near a tunnel/ bridge, and we headed up and down a big hill into *Villava*. It was a Saturday afternoon, and *Villava* appeared to be like a ghost town. Everything was closed up and the only activity was three kids playing soccer on the sidewalk in one block we passed by. It then occurred to us that it was "siesta" time. This was our first experience with this phenomenon where everything stops at about 4 pm until about 7 pm. The *Calle Mayor* stretched out for quite a while before we took a few twists and turns to head out of *Villava* past a large nursery. Greg was interested in stopping here, but we were really getting tired from the days' walk and decided to continue on. The sun had gone back in, and the clouds were once again filling up the sky. The temperature dropped by about 15 degrees within a very short time as the wind picked up. We had to go through a large park-like area for approximately two miles before coming to the river (*rio Arga*). We followed along the river for a short while until we came to the beautiful *Puente Magdalena* that led us into the fortress park that guards the city of *Pamplona*. From there it was just a short walk up into the city and to *Plaza del Castillo* where our hotel was located.

Chapter Six

Pamplona to Logrono

Day Three, Night in Pamplona

Hotel Europa is a 3-star hotel just off the *Plaza del Castillo*. By the time we climbed the stairs to the lobby registration desk, we were exhausted. As usual, our luggage was right there for us, and we made our way to the room and collapsed on the beds. We knew that dinner in the hotel was not until 9 pm that night, so we decided to wash up and then try to find another place to eat before nine. It was at this point that both Greg and I discovered that we could hardly walk. Our calf muscles were screaming at us! I got the Wi-Fi working and emailed Heather, who is a trained Registered Nurse, about our leg problems. She suggested trying to find some kind of roller apparatus that would roll out our calves. I discovered that I could accomplish the same thing by sitting at the edge of the bed and rolling my calves over the edge. This helped loosen them up. Greg did the same thing and it seemed to be quite effective.

After showers, we got dressed and headed down to the front desk. We had to use the elevator, because our legs were still killing us. The hotel clerk recommended going a few blocks south to *Calle San Nicolas* where there were several good restaurants. As we headed in that direction, we were amazed how everything had suddenly changed. It seemed as if everyone had suddenly come out of the hibernation of siesta and was out on the streets. *Calle San Nicolas* appeared to be the happening place for bars and restaurants in *Pamplona*, and every place we came to was filled to the gills.

After wandering around for ten minutes or so, we finally found a less-crowded restaurant, called '*La Chistera*'. When we stepped inside, the bar was very active, and we were told that the restaurant would not be serving until 8 pm. Well, since that was better than 9 pm, we decided to stay and have a drink while waiting. The waiter said that would be fine. He brought us some menus and we ordered a drink. Eight o'clock was now approaching, and we noticed that others were ordering dinner and some were receiving their meals by this time. We called the waiter over, and he began to speak rapidly about *"ocho hora"*, shrugging his shoulders and pointing at his watch, and then something else that I was unable to understand. We ordered another drink and sat there for an additional 15 minutes. Then we were approached by another waiter who greeted us in English and proceeded to explain the entire menu to us. As it turned out, the first waiter had been telling us that an English-speaking waiter was on the way and should be in the restaurant by 8 o'clock. The new waiter happened to be that guy, and he apologized for being late. We ordered our meal and received a bottle of *vino tinto* that was included in the €12 price for the *"menu del dia."* The appetizer consisted of pickled peppers sprinkled with sea salt. *Delicioso!*

The walk home from the restaurant was difficult due to our aching calf muscles, and the wind and rain had started which made it quite cold outside. Back at the room, we tried the massage thing on the side of the bed and it seemed to help. We then fell asleep, looking forward to a day of rest and tour of Pamplona in the morning.

Day Four, Pamplona

The breakfast buffet was served in the main dining area of the hotel, and it was quite nice, to say the least. Plenty of fresh fruit and cheese and cold cut meat. The omnipresent toast was also plentiful, along with a large selection of jams and jellies. The coffee proceeded from a special machine that required one to put a pre-selected disc in the machine — not too bad.

Greg and I discussed our plans for the day, and decided that we had two priorities before anything else. One priority was to see if we could get any laundry done and the other was to buy a phone to use for the rest of the trip.

The desk clerk told us that the laundry could be done by the hotel or there was a self-serve Laundromat right on the plaza just a block away. We decided to opt for the self serve, and we found it quite easily, thanks to good directions from the clerk. Greg and I were the only people in the place, and we found it to be a very efficient operation. While the laundry was drying, I decided to try and find the *Orange* store to buy a cell phone. Since I was able to get Wi-Fi in the Laundromat, I looked up *Orange* on the internet through my smart phone and found a store that was only about four blocks away. With map in hand, I set out to find it.

It was relatively chilly outside, and I was glad that I had dressed warmly. This consisted of a T-shirt, fleece outer shirt and my waterproof jacket. I remember thinking that if it were to get any colder, I was not prepared and would most likely have to buy something down the road. I made a mental note to check to see when the next large town was since I thought that perhaps I might be better to buy something in *Pamplona* while I was here. A few steps later, I found the *Orange* store, but it was closed. That's when I discovered that all the stores were closed. It was Sunday. Doh! The hours on the store window indicated that it would be open at 10 am on Monday. This would do us no good whatsoever, since we figured to be long-gone by that time tomorrow. Suddenly, the decision to buy a phone was made much easier. I returned to the Laundromat, and told Greg of my adventures, and we finished off the laundry and scooted back to the hotel.

The only thing left to do was to get out on the street and do some sightseeing. We headed out for the *Plaza de Toros* first and then made our way back through the winding medieval streets to the fortress that we came through the day before.

Climbing to the top of the walls, we were able to get a great view of the valleys and mountains we passed through on the way into town. On the way back to the *Plaza del Castillo* we found a small store that sold bread and meats. Greg bought a sausage and I purchased a large loaf of French bread for our journey tomorrow, feeling fairly certain that we would be able to pick up some good fruit from the breakfast buffet. On the Plaza there was a sandwich shop that was open, and we ordered a *bocadillo con jamon y queso* with a glass of wine. The sandwich was just so-so, but that did not stop us from eating it. At the very least, it would tie us over until another late dinner. Back at the hotel we took a much needed nap. When we awoke, we turned on the TV in the room just for kicks and discovered what would render many hours of enjoyment for us – Spanish Game Shows! Our favorite was one where contestants competed against each other to answer questions from the host. If they continued to answer correctly they could advance, but if they answered incorrectly enough times, the floor would open up below their feet and they fell through it and out of sight! This was hysterical to us, especially the looks on the faces of those being dropped. This show, which we never found the name of, was usually on every night at seven pm, so we were able to catch it many times since that was generally when we were waiting to go down to dinner. By now, it was nearly eight pm and we decided to go back to the same restaurant, *La Chistera*, which means Top Hat in English! The same waiter was there and he appeared delighted to see us again. He brought us extra portions of the salty pickled peppers. After dinner, the waiter brought us some homemade cordial wine that was "on the house". Another great dining experience. That was the extent of our nighttime activities since we were expecting a big day in the morning with a climb up to the *Alto del Perdon*.

On Monday morning we were able to get to the hotel restaurant for an early breakfast where we met a group of women from Washington State who were walking from *Pamplona* to *Logrono*. They left before us after saying that they hoped to see us later on down the road.

Day Five, Pamplona to Puente de la Reina

The trip out of *Pamplona* led us through city streets busy with Monday-morning traffic. We traversed the *Parc Ciudadela* and crossed under the N-240 to reach the University of *Navarre* where many students greeted us with friendly nods. Before long we were out of the city limits and climbing a long hill up the road that leads to *Cizur Menor*. From there, it was out into the open spaces and a steep climb up to the *Alto del Perdon* (Hill of Forgiveness).

During this section we began to encounter fellow pilgrims that we would see time and time again – two middle-age Germans who walked at a rather strenuous pace, a German couple, two Canadian sisters, and an Australian pilot were just some of the recurring characters that would dot the landscape for us. *Alto del Perdon* was windy beyond belief. It was next to impossible to stand still so as to take a non-blurry photo. Up to this point, the rain had held off except for a few scattered sprinkles.

At the far west of the hill, the valley opened up below and we had a spectacular view of where we were to head for the rest of the day.

The trek down the mountain validated the warnings we had from the guide book that this is where many fall, because they are not careful and attempt to move too fast. Our muscles were tired and not fully recovered from the first few days, so we heeded the warnings and managed to stay upright. At the base of the hill, we found a bench and rested for lunch. Soon, we were past *Uterga* and *Obanos* and into *Puente la Reina* and our destination for the evening, the *Hotel Jakue*.

It seemed that most of those we had seen and briefly spoken to were also staying at the *Jakue*, so dinner became a cordial social event. Greg and I had a double Scotch at the bar waiting for dinner to be served. Later, we all shared a buffet dinner and dining hall with large communal tables. Sitting to my right at the next table were the two Canadian sisters, Susan and Carrie. At breakfast, we were joined by the Australian pilot, whose name was Paul. Greg had spent a considerable time the day before talking to him along the way. Paul was walking the Camino by himself while his wife was in California visiting their daughter.

Day Six: Puente de la Reina to Estella

Not altogether uneventful, but a day with few physical challenges, and in that sense, a welcome change. We experienced short climbs up and down into the small villages of *Maneru, Cirauqui, Lorca*, and *Villatuerta*, each of which had something remarkable, be it a church or bridge that was unique.

Along the way, we saw our German friends who waved to us as we passed them and they passed us. We also encountered Susan and Carrie who always managed to stay ahead of us most of the time. We often saw them in the small villages. They were stopping for coffee and potty breaks at various bars, a common practice among many of the pilgrims. Greg and I were prone to just drinking water and using the great outdoors as our rest room. Before long, Greg was having problems with a blister on one of his toes and had to stop to make some further adjustments to his boots.

We walked for some time with a retired Irishman from *Dublin* who was quite interesting to talk to. He and two others were walking a section of the Camino, and Greg had encountered him on the very first day heading up the Pyrenees. He indicated that he was going as far as *Logrono* this trip and would take a bus from there to *Barcelona* where he would fly back to *Dublin*.

Outside of *Cirauqui*, we came upon a well-preserved section of the Old Roman Road. As we walked upon it, I began to ponder the probability that the Apostle James must have walked on this road during his time in the area nearly 2,000 years ago.

We arrived in *Estella* by late afternoon to encounter the Canadian sisters arguing in front of a large map about where their hotel was located. We consulted the map also to find our way, but this didn't last very long once we crossed over the river into the town proper. I stopped to ask directions from a woman who was sweeping her front steps. She was very pleasant, but we could only decipher a general direction from her comments. We headed that way and soon we found the narrow *Calle Mayor* and headed northeast. After a long walk through the city, we located the somewhat drab *Hotel Yerri* and checked in. Though drab and cold, this hotel was probably one of the better places in *Estella*, a town that has seen many better days for sure. Staying at the hotel was our Irish friend, Michael with whom we had walked earlier. By this time, he had been joined with the others in his party. For dinner, I had garlic soup for the first time and found it to be delicious. Pork chops and French fries were on the *"menu del dia"* along with the omnipresent *vino tinto*. By now we were discovering that the menus for dinner in these places did not vary too much. The desserts were almost always the same, with the choices being ice cream, a small cake (*torta*) of some sort, or "*flan.*" As was becoming par for the course, the Wi-Fi worked in the lobby only, and we were able to connect with Heather and Marianne via Facebook and e-mail while we sat in some rather uncomfortable chairs. By now it was about nine pm and we headed up to the room for bed.

Day Seven: Estella to Los Arcos

The wet streets indicated that there had been some substantial rain during the night. Greg and I both remarked that we had slept so soundly that neither of us heard it. The air felt cool and fresh, and the sun was beginning to peek through the buildings on our right shoulders as we made our way back through the city to the Camino across the *rio Ega*. It was here that I saw the famous steps leading up to *Iglesia San Pedro*. Time to stop for a picture of this.

As we proceeded west, I caught a glimpse of the castle ruins high above the town and began to reflect on the artistic glory that once flourished here.

Within a few minutes, we were intersecting with the N-111 at two roundabouts and then proceeded through the relatively modern suburbs to make our way towards *Irache*. Here, at the outskirts of *Estella*, we encountered once again the ladies from Washington who we had met in *Pamplona* at breakfast that last day there. While we headed up a long hill southwest of town to *Ayequi*, we got to know them a little better. It turns out that they were all members of the same church and attended a book club. Every year they challenged themselves to take a trip together to some part of the world. They had all watched the movie, *The Way*, and were inspired to come to Spain. Their trip would be a short one however, since they were walking from *Pamplona* to *Burgos* and then returning home from there. It soon became apparent that they were experienced walkers and were travelling light, with very small packs. We stayed with them for a while, but they were outpacing even Greg. I stayed behind the pack with one of the older members of the group who was moving at about the same pace as I and had a pleasant conversation.

Soon we were the *Monasterio Irache* to sample the outdoor fountain. By this time, it was quite crowded, and there were several large groups of bikers who were hogging the scene, each one wanting his picture taken drinking the wine. I decided that this was not that important to me and just snapped a quick picture and moved on.

After *Irache*, there was a steady climb up through oak and pine forests before a slight descent to *Monjardin*. Here, the countryside became more fascinating around each turn of the Camino. Crushed granite trails wound their way through lush green fields dotted with stunning patches of what I assumed was mustard -- at least, I thought it was mustard while I was walking. It was only until later, when I returned and was compiling my notes that I learned from a reader that this amazing yellow crop was indeed rapeseed, from which canola oil is made.

The rain held off for most of the day as we pushed past *Monjardin* through seemingly endless farmland with more splendid rapeseed, and then we headed down into *Los Arcos*.

Los Arcos is a small village of 1,300 with a long main street that winds through the narrow downtown. At the far outskirts of town, we found our hotel, but not before passing through the *Plaza de Santa Maria* where we saw our Washington ladies who had already been to their hotel, showered, and were now enjoying a glass of wine at an outdoor café. The sun was beginning to break through the clouds we had experienced all day, and it was indeed welcome. Greg and I checked into *Hotel Ezequiel*, got cleaned up and headed for the bar on the first floor where we shot a game of pool and had a drink. We found a lounge area that had some comfortable chairs, and we sat here and communicated with home via email. Oddly enough, there was a treadmill machine in this room. Greg thought he would use it to get some exercise in prior to dinner! Not! Before long some of our acquaintances began to appear at the hotel. First were the Canadian sisters, then the German couple and finally Paul. At dinner that night we sat with Susan, Carrie and Paul and enjoyed their company and conversation as we shared our lives at home and experiences thus far along the way.

Day Eight: Los Arcos to Logrono

Our walking notes told us that this promised to be a long and somewhat arduous day of 18 miles walking on the way to *Logrono*, so we headed out early. At the bus stop, just a few blocks from our hotel, we saw a number of pilgrims who appeared to be taking the bus to *Logrono*. We wondered why, and later we would find out. At the outskirts of town, we passed an interesting cemetery. The gates were locked, so we just moved on.

Once out on the trail, the clouds subsided and the warm sun was at our back. Within an hour or so, we had reached the classic Pilgrim town of *Torres del Rio* with its narrow and winding cobblestone streets. It was here we happened upon the wonderful *Iglesia de Santo Sepulcro*, a 12th century structure based on the church of the Holy Sepulcher in Jerusalem. We poked our heads in here and stood for a while at the back to soak in the atmosphere. It was cold and dark, but one could actually feel the crisp acoustics in the octagonal building.

From here, we had a significant climb up to *Alto N. S. del Poyo*, and then we dropped down dramatically to the *rio Cornava* and made our way slowly up to the town of *Viana*. The Camino led us right through the middle of town and we passed the beautiful *Iglesia Santa Maria*. Outside the church was the tomb of Cesare Borgia as well as the amazing in-laid sculptures of the agony of Christ.

There was another really steep descent out of *Viana* before the Camino leveled off into the *La Rioja* wine making region. At the outskirts of *Logrono*, we met up with Susan and Carrie and walked all the way into the city. This was a long slog through an industrial section before reaching the *Ebro* River and the parks that skirt the town. Susan and Carrie told us that they were planning to spend two nights in *Logrono*. We said goodbye and found our hotel (F&G) which was at the north end of town as we headed in.

F&G was a beautiful, modern hotel, and Greg and I enjoyed a respite from the more basic stuff we had been experiencing. In the bar downstairs, after a glorious shower, we had a glass of wine and made plans for dinner. The desk clerk recommended that we head to the *Plaza Mercado* for a variety of restaurants. I decided to give my feet a rest from the hiking boots and opted for the *Teva* sandals to walk around town. This turned out to be a big mistake! Trying to see a menu at one of the restaurants, I inadvertently tripped over a small curb and took a header onto the cobblestone pavement. Two Spanish girls at a nearby outside table looked on in horror. While Greg rushed over to help me, I managed to get to my feet and found that I had stubbed my toe so badly that I could hardly walk. We hobbled into a nearby café and decided to eat there, although we really couldn't understand the menu items very well. At the table, I was flooded with fear that I might be unable to continue because of this injury. Needless to say, dinner was not a very enjoyable experience that evening. Later, I limped back to the hotel and assessed the situation. It was becoming clear to me that I had very likely broken my toe. I taped it up, attaching it to my second toe to keep it as immobile as possible. After swallowing an 800 mg Ibuprofen to deaden the pain, I fell asleep hoping and praying that the morning would bring good news.

Chapter Seven

Logrono to Burgos

Day Nine: Logrono to Najera

Although I slept extremely well with the Ibuprofen, the morning did not bring good news. I found that I was unable to put any significant weight on my right foot. Knowing that the route to *Najera* would be 18 miles, much of it over lots of hardscape, Greg convinced me to take a bus to *Najera*. At the desk in the lobby, I said goodbye to Greg, who was going to walk by himself. The desk clerk called me a cab which I took to the bus station that was approximately 3 kilometers from the hotel. After purchasing a ticket at the *Logrono* bus station and sorting out the confusing departure gates, I finally found the right boarding area and got the correct bus.

The ride to *Najera* was only 20 minutes! The driver let me out in the northeast corner of town, and I found that I had to walk down through the main section of the town and cross the river at the west end to find the *Hotel Duques*. "Walking" was not an apt term for my gait — more like "limping", I would say. It was an absolutely beautiful day, with very mild temps and clear skies. It probably took me the same time to limp this distance to the hotel as it did to ride the bus all the way from *Logrono*! *Hotel Duques* turned out to be a delightful place, just 100 meters from the lovely river walk cafes.

After checking in, I informed the desk clerk that my friend would be arriving later in the afternoon, and she agreed to greet him and show him to the room. The river walk was right below where the Camino crosses the river and I decided that this would be an ideal place to sit and wait for Greg. Choosing a ham sandwich (*bocadilla con jamon*) and a beer from one of the café menus, I sat out in the sunshine and caught up on journal entries while eating. After approximately one hour the sun went in and the wind picked up so I decided to go back to the hotel room. This allowed me the opportunity to contact home via Facebook and post some pictures.

Before long, Greg arrived with his stories of the day. It appeared that there was a long 2-3 mile walk out of Logrono on busy roads that would have been misery with my foot in the shape it was currently. Along the way, Greg had been following another pilgrim who, as it turned out, had taken a wrong turn. Soon they both realized the mistake and had to back-track. Whoops! Greg admitted that he was sort of daydreaming and not thinking about where he was going. Fatal mistake on the Camino! Greg asked me for an update on my injury, and I reported that I was no worse, there appeared to be no swelling, and that I could probably walk in the morning, God willing.

The hotel desk clerk directed us to a restaurant nearby since they did not serve dinner at the hotel. The restaurant was located in the old section of town on a remote back alley and appeared to be somewhat questionable, at least from the outside. As we walked in, we noticed there were other pilgrims in the place who were enjoying their meal and having a good time. At the next table we were surprised to see Claire from Pleasanton who was eating with three other ladies! Greg and I were amazed that she made it this far. The last time we saw her she was struggling up the Pyrenees on that first day. We were certain that she had dropped out. It was a happy reunion, and we were both glad she was still in the game. The meal was quite good, and once again I had the garlic soup as my *primero*, with veal chops for *secundo*, then ice cream for dessert.

Day Ten: Najera to Santo Domingo de La Calzada

We were now deep into *La Rioja*, the premier wine-growing region in Spain, and we walked through many vineyards, lush wheat fields and more rapeseed than one could possibly imagine.

Our first stop was in *Azofra*. We plopped down on some benches in the main square and ate some fruit and nuts from our buffet at *Hotel Duques*. Along the way we had been joined from time to time by a fellow pilgrim and his dog. This sheepdog kept looking back at us until we caught up to him and then he rejoined his master ahead of us. He had his own backpack and seemed to be doing just fine with it. In *Azofra*, his master went in and bought some food for him, so he was snacking right along with us. There in the square I befriended 3 middle-aged German couples. When I told them what had happened to me in *Logrono*, they seem sympathetic. After a while, one of the men in the group came over and gave me some tape which he said would help me bandage my foot properly. I thanked him, but told him that I had some tape of my own. He acknowledged this, then smiled and the Germans moved on out of town. Little did I know at the time, but this was the first of many kindnesses that would be extended in many ways from many *peregrinos* over the course of 6 weeks.

Within an hour or so, we reached the top of a hill and encountered a rare rest-stop/picnic area. There we encountered the three German couples again, and I bantered back and forth with them. They turned out to be very jolly and friendly, and they referred to me as Mr. California. There was a funny sign at this rest stop that said "don't shit" with a figure in a squat position. Greg and I both got a significant chuckle out of this.

About half way to *Santo Domingo*, we entered the strange town of *Ciruena*. At the east of town, there was a golf club called *Rioja Alta* and just after that we passed through what appeared to be a modern ghost town—and a builder's nightmare. Dozens of newly built and unoccupied townhouses and single family homes stretched out before us. Greg and I theorized that they must have built this development on speculation and then the economy was so bad that no one moved there and bought houses. Soon we were past this section and into the older part of the town that was also fairly deserted before reaching *Santo Domingo de Calzada*. After entering the city limits, we discovered that we had a long way to walk to get to the center of town where our hotel was located. We found it and discovered that there was a middle aged French couple waiting outside unable to get in. They were also pilgrims and heading in the reverse direction. Using our combined knowledge of minimal Spanish, we used their phone and called the number listed on the outside of the building. Within five minutes, our pleasant host came and showed us to our rooms. Later we found a *mercado* a few block away and bought food for the next day and then located the recommended Italian restaurant in the main part of town for a good meal.

Day Eleven: Santo Domingo to Belorado

From the hotel, we picked up the Camino just a block away in the older section of town, and there we happened upon Claire as we were leaving town. By this time, she was hobbling along with a bad knee injury and quite concerned about her situation. We told her that we would pray for her to find a doctor and get the knee looked at. Then we headed out of town across the *rio Oja*.

What started out as a rather chilly cloudy morning turned into a beautiful sunny day within one hour. After *Granon*, it became almost hot, and for the remainder of the day, we were in shorts and t-shirts.

From the top of the hill in *Granon*, I took a "selfie" that indicated only 555km to go. We both remarked that we have made significant progress, but we were not even half way to *Santiago*. Still 350 miles to go!

Greg and I got somewhat separated before we re-united in *Vilamayor del Rio*. For the last two days, I had been walking gingerly on my right leg because the toe still hurt, and I began to discover that I was developing a blister on the left heel that would need to be treated when I got to *Belorado*.

By this time, we had crossed into the *Castilla y Leon* region, the largest autonomous region in Spain. As we checked out the large sign, we noted that we will be travelling through three of its provinces: *Burgos*, *Palencia* and *Leon*. After *Burgos*, we will have the infamous *Meseta* to look forward to. This is a flat plateau or mesa that will bring many challenges, both in weather and endurance.

Redecilla, Castildelgado, Viloria and *Villamayor* were delightful hamlets that we passed through on our journey this day, all with something different to add to the visual splendor we experienced.

After a long day in the welcome sunshine, we finally reached *Belorado* in the late afternoon. The *Hostel Verdeanco* was right on the Camino, and we found that we had another pleasant host that directed us to our rooms and told us about restaurants in the *Plaza Mayor* that he would recommend.

After a shower and a brief nap, we found that the Wi-Fi worked in the room, and so we took the time to contact home. There was definitely a blister that was growing on my left heel. I determined that this was happening due to the way I was favoring my right foot. I bandaged it up as well as I could, using what I had in my first aid kit, and then prayed for the best. Later, we explored the nearby *Plaza Mayor* and found a restaurant to have a beer and then a good dinner.

Day Twelve: Belorado to San Juan de Ortega

The day started out with an adventure just at the western outskirts of town. Near our hotel, we ran into the German couple, Hermann and Gerta that we had met near *Roncesvalles*. As we crossed the main street heading west, a car veered off the road and appeared to be coming right at us. Gerta did not see it, so I grabbed her backpack and pulled her out of the way. She was startled but thanked me profusely. As it turned out, the driver was only pulling into a driveway that was on our left and as he did so, he indicated that he was somewhat irritated that we were in his way. It became apparent that pedestrians did not have the right of way in this part of the world. I remembered that the Brierley guide book continually reminded folks that it was dangerous near the roads, and now I had first-hand knowledge.

Before we reached *Tosantos*, we came upon a pilgrim couple that was travelling with their two children and riding donkeys. This made for some unique pictures. The first part of the day involved a gradual climb through hilly farmland for about 7 miles until we reached the village of *Villafranca Montes de Oca*.

It was here that Greg and I stopped for lunch in a small café and then found at the west end of town a good place to rest and air out our feet and changed our socks to prepare for the long climb to follow. As usual, Greg was well ahead of me within a few minutes and I struggled up a very steep path where I encountered two bicyclists who were carrying their road bikes on their shoulders. They were breathing hard and sweating profusely at this arduous task. I made a lame joke about not riding up the hill, and they just stared at me and mounted their bikes at the top of the incline and rode away to join a downhill path that led to the N-120 a short way below us. I kept moving up the hill to reach the *Mojapan* rest stop and then further up to the *Monumento a los Caidos,* a stark monument to the fallen fighters during the Spanish Civil War.

After about an hour, I realized that I was now deep in the middle of the **black forest of** *Monte de Oca*, and I was unquestionably hurting physically and undoubtedly beginning to feel afraid of my surroundings. It had only been four days earlier that I had broken my right toe in that fall in the city of *Logrono*, and it was becoming increasingly difficult to walk; however, I had devised a method of a half-step on the bad foot that would later prove to be somewhat disastrous.

For over an hour now I had been walking completely alone. Proceeding upwards, I eventually reached a flat spot and passed through a solitary stretch of wide path that appeared to be cut like a fire road. On either side there were foreboding black pine forests that were so thick I could only see about fifty feet in before they receded into darkness. The day was stretching on now, and the solitude was beginning to have an effect on me. By this time the clouds had come in and the temperature appeared to have dropped by 15 degrees at least. With each turn in the trail, I thought I might be finally beginning the descent into *San Juan de Ortega*, but indeed another turn or unexpected uphill presented itself. It was now over two hours on this lonely trek, seeing no other person. It then occurred to me that I had not seen a trail marker in quite some time either. Once again, fear began to enter my consciousness. Had I taken a wrong turn somewhere? Was this why I had seen no one for this long period of time?

In the distance, I could hear the sound of a car, and then suddenly, speeding around a corner of the dirt road ahead of me, was the most un-expected sight – a beat-up sedan was heading my way. The car was careening from side to side, almost out of control. I moved to the side of the road as the car got nearer, not knowing what to think of this strange occurrence. When it was almost upon me, the car slowed down perceptibly and I was now able to see the occupants – two in the front and two in the back – all young men in their late teens it appeared. The windows were wide open and they were staring wild-eyed at me as they passed by. It was apparent that they were either crazed or drugged up, perhaps both. I could see them gesturing wildly and arguing with one another as they sped on. I decided not to look back at them for too long, for fear this might incite some senseless reaction from them. The car took a sharp turn to the left about 50 yards past me and disappeared down another dirt road that I now remembered passing just a few moments ago. At this point, I knew that it was time to make a decision of what to do next. Should I head into the woods to take cover, perhaps to disappear from sight if they decided to return? Or would it be more dangerous in the woods, harder for me to navigate with the bad foot and basically impossible to elude them in that environment should they pursue me, and also giving them more cover to beat and rob me? Also, what would I encounter in those woods in the form of creatures that would be equally harmful? I decided to keep moving quickly forward on the trail as best I could, all the while listening for the sound of the car engine. If the sound grew louder, I would make a run for the woods and hide. The next few moments were critical since I didn't want them to see me heading for cover. I would need enough time to cross the open grassy area of about 30-40 yards before making it into the woods. Way off, I could hear the engine rev up briefly but then appear to be getting further away. It was now a fairly safe bet that they had decided to keep going towards the main road, the N-120, which went east to *Villafranca* or west to *Burgos*. I adjusted my panicked pace somewhat and began to pray the Jesus Prayer fervently. "Lord Jesus Christ, Son of God, have mercy on me, a sinner." I repeated the prayer over and over. After a few moments, I noticed that my pace had picked up quite appreciatively, and I was no longer feeling any pain. It felt as if my feet were hardly touching the ground. The Lord preserved me. After a while, the trail narrowed a bit and I looked down for some reason to see a small black adder making its way across to the other side. I grabbed my smart phone, pressed the camera icon, chased the adder until I could get a good picture, and snapped. Greg and I had been warned about indigenous poisonous snakes before we left, but up until this time had not seen any. The adder slithered away into the grass at the edge of the trail, and I secured my phone in my pants pocket. Within a hundred yards, the trail went through a clearing and opened up to a long downhill that crossed a small brook. After that I could see that it went sharply up again. Ahead of me I could see a biker joining the trail after the brook and then stopping about half way up the next hill at an object at the side of the trail. As I continued down, the biker moved away from the object and disappeared over the hill. I wondered what the object might be. I looked as if it might be an abandoned sleeping bag. As I got closer, the object got clearer and it was now obvious that this was a person lying at the side of the trail. Within a minute or so, I could see that the person was indeed my walking buddy, Greg! He was just lying there resting. I pulled out my smart phone and suggested that he might not want to be lying on the ground after he saw what I was going to show him. The rest of the way into St. John of the Nettle, we had a lot to talk about.

From this point we were only forty minutes or so from San Juan. The wind was picking up once again and it looked as if it would rain any minute. There was a steep descent into *San Juan de Ortega*. Once there, we found that there was one hotel, one bar and one *alberque* in the tiny village with a population of 30. We would later discover that these establishments were all owned by the same family. We found the *La Henera Hotel* easily at the entrance to town, and there on the front door was a posted sign that stated that we had to go to the *Bar Marcela* to check in. We walked the hundred meters to the bar and where we were given a key to the front door and our room. While Greg was in the shower, there was a knock at the door and there stood a man with two plastic bags. He gave them to me and said only: "Breakfast, senor". We soon found out there was no Wi-Fi in the hotel or anywhere in town for that matter. There was however a bus stop across from *Bar Marcela* and next to that was an "internet café". This was actually two ancient computers in a hut alongside the road. For €2 we could get online for 5 minutes. Greg joked that the PC looked like a *Commodore 64*, and it nearly was this old. I used Greg's Facebook account and messaged that we had arrived safely and were incommunicado for the rest of the day.

The Bar Marcela was beginning to serve meals, but it was so crowded because of the attached *alberque* occupants that the wait was going to be long. This did not seem to phase the occupants stuffed into the bar who were well into their third or fourth round already. We decided to go back to our room and wound up eating some of our breakfast provisions for the next day. We knew, from our notes, that the next day would be a tough trek into Burgos, and we definitely needed the rest.

Day Thirteen: San Juan de Ortega to Burgos

It was a wet morning getting out of *San Juan*, and after an hour or so, the clouds cleared off. We had both slept well and were energized for the day. There was a strenuous climb west of *Atapuerca*, but from there the rest of the day was a gentle walk through the valley of the *rio Vena*. After *Obaneja*, Greg and I decided to take the shorter route into *Burgos* towards the north. This involved a long slog through an industrial area southwest of the airport.

This seemingly endless walk along *Calle Vitoria* eventually brought us into the main part of the city near the *Museo Militar*. We should have headed north at that point and followed the Camino on *Calle Las Calzades* but instead, for some reason, we missed that turn and kept near the river until we reached *Calle Garcia*. Getting some directions from a passing resident, we tried to follow where she told us to go, and that just confused us further. Eventually we found our way to *Plaza San Lesmes* and from there to *Arco San Juan*.

A block or so later we arrived at *Hotel Cordon* where we would stay for a couple of nights. We were greeted by a very friendly staff that made us welcome. The *Hotel Cordon* on *Calle de la Puebla* was a pleasant "three-star" just one-half block from the *Plaza de la Libertad* and the *Casa Cordon*.

It was here in this plaza, 516 years ago, that Queen Isabella welcomed Christopher Columbus back from his discovery of the New Land. The hotel had no in-house restaurant, save for the small dining area towards the back of the lobby that was used for breakfast, but the evening desk clerk spoke excellent English, and he directed us to a vicinity nearby the hotel where we would be able to find great places to eat. We found the bustling area on a couple of narrow streets near

Plaza Mayor and settled on *Restaurante Pancho* on *San Lorenzo*. This proved to be an excellent choice, and the *Rioja* wine we had with the meal was truly outstanding. Tomorrow would be a day of rest and touring the city.

Day Fourteen: A Day in Burgos

After a delicious breakfast, the desk clerk directed us to an area where we might find a self-serve laundry. After a cursory search that lasted about one hour we decided to go back to the hotel and avail ourselves of the hotel laundry services. This would cost us about ten dollars, but we didn't want to spend any more valuable time in these pursuits. We set out for the Cathedral about ten thirty and walked to the *rio Arlanzon* where we found the *Disputacion Provincial* and the statue of *El Cid*.

From there it was a short walk through groomed Mulberry trees to the *Arco de Santa Maria* that led to the great plaza in front of the Cathedral. We entered the Cathedral from the west end only to find that the main entrance was on the south side. It was here that we purchased entry tickets and tour headphones. After finding the channel in English, we set out to view this massive structure in a somewhat organized way. Greg's headphones were not working properly so he went back to exchange them. It was then that I lost contact with him in the crowd, so I finished touring the Cathedral on my own. Within five minutes, I discovered that the guided tour was a hindrance to me, and I turned the recording off completely, preferring instead to just walk and absorb this beautiful space. There seemed to be no restriction on picture taking as there was in Notre Dame, so I was able to take quite a lot of shots.

In two hours I had finished the tour with no sign of Greg along the way. I left the building, returning my headphones and looked to see if he might be waiting outside. Again, there was no sign of him, so I sat on one of the plaza benches positioned to see anyone coming out of the exit. After a half hour of observing some young Spanish students cavorting around in the plaza, I decided to head back to the hotel. Back at the room, our laundry had been returned to us and was laid out completely folded on the beds. The separate bags that we had left at the desk earlier, had been combined in the wash and were all together, grouped carefully by the chambermaid into shirts, pants, socks and underwear. I pulled out my things and left the rest neatly arrayed on Greg's bed. I headed back to Cathedral square and searched the area for any sign of Greg.

No luck! *The Plaza Mayor* was another great place to sit and watch people which I did for about 30 minutes – then back to the hotel to take a nap. Greg had still not returned, but within a few minutes the door rattled and he entered, surprised as I was at the laundry display. He too was feeling exhausted and wanted a nap as well. I posted some pictures on Facebook and dozed off, waking up to the sound of the shower in the bathroom. I turned on the TV and found our favorite game show. Greg joined the fun a few minutes later and we both howled at the crazy contestants being dropped from their circle! Soon it was time to eat. After stopping at a department store (*El Corte Ingles*) and a bank to withdraw some cash at the ATM, we found a restaurant that we had seen advertised earlier that served American food. For some reason that really appealed to us at this juncture of the trip, and we ordered a big cheeseburger and fries, topping it off with chocolate sundaes for desert. The only drawback to this dining experience was a group of school children at a birthday party in a room at the restaurant that was raucous and really irritating to both of us. The parents couldn't control them, but fortunately they left somewhat early after about two bites of our meal. Then it was back to the hotel and to sleep as we would head towards the *Meseta* tomorrow.

Chapter Eight

Burgos to Fromista

Day Fifteen: Burgos to Hornillos

At breakfast in the hotel, we met a chap from California who was doing the Camino on a mountain bike. It was interesting getting his perspective of the experience from that angle. Both Greg and I felt like staying in *Burgos* for another day, or at least lingering awhile longer this morning, but we knew that there was a long day ahead, and the weather already looked somewhat threatening from the windows inside the hotel. Time to pack up and get underway. We got our bags down to the lobby area and set out into the city to find the Camino and head west towards *Hornillos*.

We picked up the Camino easily, and by the time we were passing the Cathedral, the rain started coming down. We stopped to poncho up and talked to some fellow pilgrims that were doing the same, but were then moving down to the Cathedral to see it for the first time. Just then our bicycle friend from breakfast happened by and waved to us. Going through *Arco de San Martin*, the rain was really coming down hard, but by the time we got to *Hospital del Rey* and the University there, it had let up some. Just past the juncture to *Villabilla*, the rain picked up again and we saw some pilgrims seeking shelter under a large tunnel that went beneath one of the major highways. We kept moving, crossing the A-231 towards *Tardajos*. It was here that we had planned to stop and eat lunch that would consist of fruit and bread scavenged from the hotel. Just into town, we found a shelter that was actually a bus waiting area, and we hunkered into this place to get out of the rain and eat.

In *Rabe de las Calzados*, we stopped at a small café/bar and ordered a coke which we took to an outside table, since the rain had let up briefly. The bartender was quite rude to me, and I could not figure out why. He just seemed irritated in general. While at the table, we observed a young American girl that we had seen from time to time. At first she was moving quickly and easily on the Camino, but now she was struggling with a major limp. I had tried to engage her in conversation in previous encounters, but she was not interested. This was just one of many younger people that we encountered along the way who seemed to start out invincible but found that this trek was far more strenuous than they had expected. They were hobbled with pulled muscles and blisters by now. We went at a slower, more deliberate pace and rested often. After *Rabe*, we climbed up onto the *Meseta* and the rain came down again.

Greg moved out ahead on the hill up and soon I lost sight of him. I continued slogging along the muddy trail. All this time I was thinking about how we would find our hotel later on. Our notes told us that when we got to *Hornillos* we were to call the hotel owner whose place was in the town of *Isar*, about three kilometers to the north. He would then come and pick us up. Since we had no telephone, we were going to have to find a café and ask the bartender there to call for us. This was going to be a challenge, given my poor Spanish, but somehow we would get through it. This was one of the more-lonely days for me, because once I was up on the *Meseta*, I was generally walking alone with no one around for about two hours. Eventually, the Camino dipped down and led into a long 3 kilometer finish into *Hornillos*.

When I entered the town, I was wet and tired. After a block or so I saw Greg who was talking to two fellow pilgrims. As it turned out, they were a middle-aged Irish couple who were more than happy to dial up our hotel number for us with their cell phone. The woman handed the phone to me and I talked with out host who spoke rudimentary English. He said he would be there in approximately ten minutes to pick us up. We continued the conversation with the Irish couple who told us they had been on the Camino previously. The wife had experienced a severe injury and they had to quit and return home. Now she had been completely rehabilitated and they wanted to come back and finish. We thanked the couple again as our host pulled up, loaded our packs and took us away to *Isar*.

The three kilometer trip to the hotel was exceedingly short since our driver had a lead foot, to say the least. I was in the front seat holding on for dear life. But we got there safely and screeched to a halt outside a delightful *casa rural* that had been recently upgraded into a very pleasant hotel. After registering, we were shown our room that was quite spacious, and we began the tedious task of getting our wet stuff off, finding a method of drying everything, and then trying to warm up from the cold and wet day. There were radiators in the room that we used to get our shoes dry by turning them upside down and placing them on top. The rest of the things we wrung out as best as possible so they wouldn't drip on the floor, and then hung up all over the room on anything that might suffice. The bath consisted of a large tub with a shower hose, but we had plenty of hot water, and we both took long showers and warmed up. I went downstairs to access the Wi-Fi since it did not work in the room.

I ordered a beer at the bar and had some pleasant conversation with the owner and his wife as well as a local patron who appeared to be a regular. They were cordially amused and interested that I came from California. Then I moved to a table so that I could post some pictures and email Heather. Before long, I was joined by a fellow pilgrim who was staying in the hotel. I invited her to sit at the table with me, and we struck up a conversation. Her name was Frida and she was from Denmark. She was a Nurse Anesthetist and was only on a two-week holiday. She had been to the Camino before and completed a different section each time – something I was to find quite common among Europeans. She left after about ten minutes or so to take care of things in her room and vowed to see us later that evening at dinner. I stayed and tried to read the news from home via the internet on my smart phone. Soon Greg came down and we had a drink in the dining room. Our jovial host then brought us a special drink of a liquor that he had made himself and poured a generous amount for each of us. It was on the house, and it was quite good. By this time, we were fully recovered from the long, wet day, and we both felt great and extremely hungry. To our delight, dinner was to be served early at seven o'clock. We left the dining area and returned to the room to check on our drying clothes. Before long, it was time to eat, and we hurried down to the dining room. There was a French couple staying at the hotel also, and I had a brief conversation with them in French. They were already eating and having a great meal it appeared. Frida came down and we invited her to join us at our table. Frida told us about her family. She was unmarried but she had a sister who had teenage children who Frida treated as her own and saw them often. She was very involved in their lives. She also gave us an inside view of the Danish health system that we both found quite interesting as we compared it to what was coming down the pipe for us with Obamacare. So, it was a great evening, making new friends and having good fellowship and food. Back in the room, our clothes and shoes were drying well and we were certain that we would have a good day tomorrow. We would be back on the *Meseta*.

Day Sixteen: Hornillos to Castrojeriz

Our host was quite cheery this morning after breakfast and carried our bags down to the car to bring us back to *Hornillos*. When we got there, he dropped us off at the far end of town where the trail picked up towards *Castrojeriz*. This probably saved us five minutes or so, and we thanked him for a very enjoyable evening. He said goodbye and wished us well. Within a few minutes we were back up onto the *Meseta*. The weather was beautiful by 9:00 am, but it became apparent that we were going to have a muddy day because of all the rain the previous days. Greg and I were soon separated, but we had agreed that we would meet for lunch in *Hontanas*, about at the halfway point.

Before long, I found that the trail was so muddy and impassable that pilgrims ahead of me had begun to forge a path along the side through the wheat fields. This often required climbing up a slippery hill to get up on that part of the new trail after I crossed a road or a canal. On a couple of occasions, I fell down and landed in the mud. I also noticed that the mud was sticking to my boots and building up about two inches. I found a cement guard around one of the canals and did the best I could to scrape the mud off. It occurred to me that my walking sticks would have been valuable in accomplishing this, but that morning I had made the decision not to carry them any longer and packed them away in my large bag that was already being transported to the next town. The mud was also slowing me down and I was not making good time to get to *Hontanas*, but I figured that Greg would wait for me as he always did. This was another spot where I found myself alone for a considerable amount of time. In spite of the difficulty walking, I found the solitude in these open wheat fields to be quite exhilarating. After *San Bol*, the *Meseta* continued on for another five kilometers and then there was a steep descent into *Hontanas*, a charming town directly on the Camino. I found Greg there sitting at a cafe, and we decided to order a pizza from the bar and eat outside at one of the tables on the main street.

It was here in *Hontanas* that we met some new friends. Sitting at the next table were two women, one of whom we had seen continually since *Estella*. Her name was Priscilla, and she was from Australia. She was walking with a friend she had met on the Camino whose name was Paulina. Paulina was Swiss and spoke perfect English. Also sitting at a table across the street was Frida, who we had met in *Hornillos*.

Frida had been moving at a quick pace. She asked us to take her picture with her full pack. It was then that we saw how big and heavy her pack was. Greg and I were both amazed at how fast this little person could go with such a huge pack. Soon she was off and headed for *Castrojeriz*. We continued talking to Paulina and Priscilla, and Greg had some back and forth with Paulina about Swiss sense of humor. It did not go over well with Paulina. As we left town, we encountered a very strange statue that everyone was taking a picture of, a "peeing man." I was no exception.

As we left *Hontanas*, the *Meseta* stretched out ahead of us once again and we came around a curve in the trail to see a herd of sheep with their shepherd and an amazing sheep dog. There were also some stone pilings that were quite interesting and we soon discovered that this was a very common sight out here on the *Meseta*.

By this time Priscilla and Paulina had caught up with us and over the next couple of hours we would see them often. We also saw two young French girls who appeared to be really enjoying their walk. When I passed them, I noticed that there were walking in sandals. Before long we reached *San Anton* and its magnificent ruins.

Castrojeriz was three miles down the road, and we arrived about three o'clock. Near the entrance to the town we saw Priscilla and Paulina ahead of us, but lost them when we stopped to talk to a man who had a strange lizard on the end of a stick. He was a rather odd fellow, but pleasant enough, who wanted us to know that he had rescued the lizard from sure death by transferring him to a water trough at the outskirts of town. As we walked through the long narrow main street of this small town of 600, we suddenly heard two voices calling to us from a second-story window. It was Susan and Carrie, our Canadian friends, who had arrived an hour or so earlier. They were in the process of doing their laundry in the hotel there and were going to be looking for a place to eat dinner later. We told them where we were staying, and they said they would try to find us and maybe have dinner.

When we got to the central section of *Castrojeriz*, we were having some difficulty finding our hotel. It was there we saw the two young French girls who told me that they couldn't find an *alberque* that had room. They were being hassled by a Spanish waiter at one of the street cafes, who said he wanted to help them find something. The girls were somewhat skeptical of this assistance, but the waiter backed off when I began talking to the girls. After a brief conversation in French, the girls indicated that they would probably move on to the next town to see if there was some place to stay there. This was a story I heard repeated over and over again by many pilgrims who were on the Camino. Greg and I were concerned about their safety, but they seemed to be confident that they would be OK.

Soon we located the street the hotel was on, according to our notes, and when we arrived, Priscilla was standing outside a nearby restaurant and informed us that the hotel was just up the street, but all the meals were served in the restaurant/bar where she was. We thanked her and checked into the hotel. After showers and doing some laundry maintenance, we ventured out to the street and down to the bar/restaurant. We got our pilgrim passports stamped at the bar and ordered a beer. Within five minutes, Susan and Carrie showed up and soon after, Priscilla. Priscilla had a drink with us, but said she would not join us for dinner. Paulina, it turned out, was tired and was staying in her room. We went downstairs into the restaurant and found a table.

In a few minutes, the two German guys we had met in Pamplona entered. We laughed with them for a bit and they found their own table. Carrie and Susan told us about their adventures in various places and about Paul who was still on the trail. They had seen a lot of him, but had lost track after *Logrono*. We had a good meal and laughed a lot about our experiences thus far. Carrie said that they were proud of themselves for all the conversions they were making. They were talking about converting folks over to staying in hotels as opposed to the *alberques*. Susan also told us about her husband, Bruce. Their 40th wedding anniversary was coming up in a few days, and she was getting clues that he might be joining them somewhere along the way, just because of the questions she was getting from him via email. Carrie was certain that this was going to happen, but Susan was just as certain it would not. They told us they would be staying in *Castrojeriz* for an additional day so we would not be seeing them for a while. We said goodbye and headed to our hotel for a good night sleep.

Day Seventeen: Castrojeriz to Fromista

Another beautiful morning to come down out of *Castrojeriz* and then way up to the *Meseta* again and the drop down into the Tierra de Campos before we get to *Fromista*. Before we left, we experienced a good breakfast in the same restaurant that we had dinner and, as usual, scavenged some food for later in the day.

After crossing the *rio Odrilla* just outside of town, we climbed the strenuous hill up to *Alto Mostelares*. On the way up I met a couple from the US who were part of a tour group. They were only going from *Burgos* to *Leon*. The woman walked with me as we struggled up the long climb. She was a teacher from NYC and had decided to come on the Camino after seeing the movie (one of many we were to meet). When we reached the top, Greg was there and we stopped to eat some fruit and drink some water before moving on. After a brief rest we continued up onto the mesa and discovered around the bend a phenomenal view of the valley below. We were looking out on the *Tierra de Campos* (The Land of Fields).

The drop down from here was substantial, but welcome after the long climb up. Within the hour we were passing the *Ermita de San Nicholas* and then across the *rio Pisuerga* over a marvelous Romanesque bridge.

There was a long walk along an irrigation canal that eventually led into the town of *Fromista*. Along the way, we could hear the intriguing sounds of various wildlife, frogs and birds, but we never really saw any to speak of.

By the time we reached *Fromista*, the temperature had soared into the eighties and we were hot. We found the hotel easily and checked in, looking forward to hot shower and a good meal. I went downstairs to check out the scene in the lobby and ran into Frida, our friend from Denmark. She was trying to find an ATM, and I went with her to accomplish this. When we got back to the hotel, she said she wanted to buy me a drink to repay me for the wine at dinner in *Hornillos (Isar)*. I accepted and ordered a beer and we sat out on the patio in front of the hotel for a really nice relaxing drink. Greg joined us shortly, and then we all walked up to a local *mercado* to buy some food for the next day. Frida was staying at another hotel, so she said goodbye and "see you on the Camino" and Greg and I went inside to see if we could eat early. To our delight, this was possible. We had a good meal, replete with the requisite wine and then went back to the room to email and Facebook and to bed.

Chapter Nine

Fromista to Sahagun

Day Eighteen: Fromista to Carrion de los Condes

I was slow getting going this morning and Greg took off ahead of me. There was a group of Italian ladies, perhaps 10 or more, who must have come in during the later hours last night. They were all walking together with small daypacks and walking sticks. They asked me if I would take a picture of them all together. After doing this, I found the way out of town and passed the *Iglesia San Martin* while obtaining some good pictures of this 12th century Romanesque church.

Soon I was crossing the busy A-67 and starting out on the "Souless *Senda*", a boring crushed granite path along side the main road heading west towards *Carrion de los Condes*. At *Poblacion de Campos*, there is an interesting playground where Greg was waiting.

There is also a small bridge across the *rio Ucieza* and a choice for the pilgrim to make about the route ahead. An itinerant pastor was on hand near the playground and the *Ermita de San Miguel* to stamp our passports and wish us well. After having a snack in the playground, Greg and I decided to follow the more direct route and stay on the *Senda* alongside the road.

After a few hours we arrived in *Villalcazar de Sirga* and passed by another magnificent Templar church of *Santa Maria la Virgin Blanca*. Three miles later we got to *Carrion de Los Condes* in the early afternoon. There was good amount of Sunday church activity in this bustling town. We wound our way through all of this to the far end of town and crossed the *rio Carrion* to *San Zoilo* where we found our hotel located in the *Real Monasterio de San Zoilo*. This was a beautiful hotel that quickly lived up to the promotional material we had seen from our notes. The room was luxurious and the bathroom spacious, two things that were greatly appreciated after a long slog along that *Senda*.

Greg and I decided to venture back across the river to the main town to see if we could find a restaurant that was open early so that we could eat. This was a lost cause. There were no *mercados* open either, to stock up for tomorrow, so it looked as if we would be "stuck" with the accommodations at the hotel. Back within the confines of *San Zoilo*, we found the bar and enjoyed a couple of beers. While sitting in the bar, I first began to notice a soreness on my right heel that I feared was a new blister developing. Upon returning to the room, I discovered that this was indeed the case. Favoring my left foot for the blister there, I was walking un-naturally and had developed a new blister on the other foot. Not good news. I re-treated the blisters as best as I could and joined Greg in the lobby while we waited for dinner hour. By the time the restaurant opened up it was 8:00 pm and we were starved. To our surprise, the French couple we had met in *Hornillos* was already seated at the next table, so we had a pleasant reunion with them. Soon we were surprised to see Frida who was staying in the hotel, not eating dinner, but was anxious to track us down and say goodbye. This we did and wished her well. After ordering dinner, The Irish couple from *Hornillos*, who had let us use their phone entered the dining room and sat near us. We were happy to see them also. They were on their way to *Calzadilla* the next day so we agreed to hook up there the following evening. Back in the room that night, we opened the window to let in some natural breeze, but there was a wedding party going on down in the bar/patio area that was playing techno-pop non stop. That was driving me crazy and we had to shut the window in order to get to sleep.

Day Nineteen: Carrion de los Condes to Calzadilla de la Cueza

The breakfast in the morning was sumptuous and we were able to stock up as planned. Soon, we were out across the omnipresent N-120 into the countryside and onto the *Via Aquitana*, built over 2000 years ago. Walking on this seemingly endless road through the countryside gave me another opportunity to contemplate the probability that the Apostle James had to have walked here if he was in the region, because this was the only road there was at the time.

Greg and I stayed together for most of the day and stopped to eat at a roadside picnic table after about four hours. This also gave us an opportunity to get our boots off and dry our socks in the bright sunshine and let our sore feet get some air. My blisters were getting worse, so I added some additional tape across them for extra padding. I planned to visit a *Farmacia* when I arrived in *Sahagun* to see if I could get any remedies that might help. I was moving slowly, so Greg took off ahead and soon I lost sight of him.

Three hours later, a gradual downward hill brought me in to *Calzadilla*. At a water fountain on the outskirts of town, I found Greg sitting there talking to some fellow pilgrims from Massachusetts — a mother and her adult daughter, who were both nurses. They thought Greg looked like Harrison Ford, and we all joked about that. He wouldn't hear the end of that for a couple of days. Another young woman was also at the fountain and appeared to be on the verge of heat stroke. Greg advised her to get some lighter clothing on and go to shorts if she were going any further. Soon everyone was on the way. Within minutes, we located our hotel on the back side of *Calzadilla*. The place was buzzing, because it was the only game in town. Just up the road was the *alberque* that was also owned by the same family. We checked into the room and found that the Wi-Fi worked only downstairs. Time to tell everyone back home that we were fine. After showers, I headed to the bar and accomplished my Facebook posts there while enjoying a cold beer. Soon the Irish couple showed up, and I asked if I could buy them a drink to finally thank them for the use of their phone a few days ago. They graciously consented and we enjoyed a good time of fellowship. They recounted their adventures along the trail the past year and what they had experienced this year. Pat told me about his blister experiences from last year. In *Santo Domingo*, there was a local "blister doctor" in one of the *alberques* who was treating everyone for donations. Pat said that he received a great treatment of lancing and bandaging that saved him for the rest of the walk, until of course his wife suffered her knee injury. I began to think that I might need the same treatment, but where would I find it?

When it was dinner time, we were all herded into a main dining room to sit at long tables and given a choice of a fish or meat dish. Greg and I sat across the table from each other and to my left was an Austrian guy who was quite conversational. He had limited English and his companion spoke no English. Once again, my German came in handy and we had an interesting conversation about Ancient-Future Faith. He was fascinated by the experiences we had in the formation of our church in Sacramento. I gave him some information about our web site and invited him to visit there to get more information. To my right was an Australian man who introduced himself as Robert. When he found out that I was American, he told me that they, the Australians, had our back in the war. I thanked him, thought of asking him "which one?", but he was involved in another conversation to his right with some other Aussies and a girl from Norway. After dinner, people filtered out to the bar and kept the party going. Greg and I hit the sack and had no trouble getting to sleep, as usual.

Day Twenty: Calzadilla to Sahagun

Another good breakfast, served to us in the busy bar area. Substantial cups of coffee and refills were a welcome surprise. The Irish couple ate with us and headed out early. Greg and I kept our fruit for later in the day and eventually got going at approximately 9:00 am. At the first cafe/bar we came to, there were several pilgrims from the *alberque* who were stopped for coffee and snacks. It was there we saw Robert from the night before accompanied by the Norwegian girl and her two dogs! We kept going on to *Ledigos* and *Terradillos de los Templarios* before stopping in *Moratinos* to eat our lunch. This time we were on the other side of the road, but it was the same long straight slog.

I had to stop and rest for a while, and Greg kept going. Once again, I lost sight of him within ten minutes. Just after crossing into the province of *Leon*, leaving *Palencia* behind, the trail took a twist near the busy highway and eventually headed to the right along the *rio Valderaduey*. I was soon led by a path along the river to a shrine called *Virgen del Puente* that consisted of some old ruins. Leaving the shrine behind, the path turned into an industrial approach to the city of *Sahagun*. At this point, I was limping considerably due to the painful blisters. Soon the entrance to the town was before me, and I crossed the city streets, map in hand, trying to find my hotel. I was so tired at this point that it was difficult to step up or down off a curb. Passing a cafe, I saw Greg sitting there where he was having a drink with a pilgrim we had met in *Villacazar*. I didn't want to stop and indicated that I really needed to get to the hotel as fast as possible. I took some wrong turns, but found it soon. Greg was there when I arrived, having taken another route. We checked in at the *Hotel El Ruedo* and carried our bags up a long stairway. The Wi-Fi only worked downstairs in the bar area, so today it was somewhat annoying. After showers, I discovered that Priscilla was also staying there and that Paulina was also in town at another hotel. Priscilla said that she would round up Paulina and see us later. Outside at the front of the hotel on the plaza, the two German guys were having their usual large beer and smoking cigars. They were happy to see me. I thought this might be a good time to go to the *Farmacia* and get some blister remedy. Two doors down form the hotel I found one! The pharmacist directed me to a section that had all kinds of bandages and tape. She also gave me some disinfectant salve that she said would be helpful to prevent infection to the *"ampollas"*. There were two American women in the store who were sympathetic to my situation. Later outside on the plaza, we conversed with them. One was a seasoned pilgrim from Asheville, North Carolina who was part of a walking club. This was her third Camino. The other woman was suffering from an injury and had been to a doctor earlier. He told her she needed to get off her feet for a couple of days, so she was going to take a bus to Leon and stay in a hotel there and then try to carry on. After a ten-minute conversation, we parted and Greg and I walked down to the far end of the *Plaza Mayor* and found an ATM where we "cashed up". Back near the hotel we ran into Priscilla who told us that

Paulina was not feeling well and was going to stay in her room. The three of us found an outfitting store, where Greg looked for a hat and Priscilla found some walking sticks that she thought would be great for Paulina. Greg didn't find a suitable hat, so we left and found a restaurant near the hotel where all three of us went inside had a great meal. After the meal, I had an email from Heather indicating that it was probably wise not to break the blisters because they might get infected. I was really torn as to what treatment I should use.

Chapter Ten

Sahagun to Leon

Day Twenty-One: Sahagun to El Burgo Ranero

Breakfast was served in the bar area of the hotel and it was surprisingly good. At one of the tables was a fellow pilgrim from Seattle who considered himself an expert on blisters. He had been talking to Greg earlier and Greg mentioned to him that I was having problems with blisters. This guy was absolutely firm that the blisters had to be broken and drained and then bandaged carefully, etc. He also said that it was better to stay off them for a while. This was not an option for me, however and I decided to listen to Heather and perhaps seek medical attention when we got to the next town. We set out about 9:00 am and easily picked up the Camino at the south-western section of the town. I stopped to take some pictures of the *Arco San Benito* and the *San Tirso* church next to it.

While at the *Arco*, we ran into the woman from North Carolina and she walked with us for a short time out of town, across the *Puente Romana* and west along the N-120 until the trail split into the *Real Camino Frances* and the older *Via Romana*.

Greg and I took the turn to the left towards *El Burgo Ranero* and once again we were on a boring and merciless *Senda*. It was threatening rain all day, and we had some brief sprinkles here and there. At a rest stop, we had another chance to see some interesting graffiti.

It was a relatively short day for us and we reached *El Burgo Ranero* mid afternoon. Our hotel was more like a motel on the busy A-231. It was attached to a large truck station and appeared to be relatively new with a diner-like bar on the bottom floor and a large dining room towards the rear.

The Wi-Fi worked well in the room. Greg took the opportunity to Skype Marianne, and I could see that he was really happy to talk to her face to face. After showers we headed down to the bar area for a drink and to wait until dinner was served in the dining room. Soon, the doors flung open and they appeared to be ready for us. Greg and I were the only table that had more than one person at it. All the other tables were single men. I figured that this really was a truck stop, and all these guys were truckers who ate quickly, drank fast and got out of there. Several of them started dinner way after us and finished long before we did. Earlier, while sitting in the bar, I took the time to familiarize myself with Spanish food terminology and figured how mistaken I was to think that my knowledge of Mexican food would suffice in Spain. Not the case at all. Tonight I had a good steak along with the omnipresent fried potatoes. Desert was ice cream, as usual, in a small paper cup. In the morning, Greg's refusal of coffee was misunderstood as a refusal of breakfast entirely and we couldn't correct that so we just ate some fruit we had in the room and got an early start.

Day Twenty-Two: El Burgo Ranero to Mansilla de las Mulas

The mini-store next to the bar area supplied us with food for the day along with a few items we thought might be helpful. We loaded up and took off for *Mansilla*. In the early hours, the trail was bleak and cold with a strong wind that lowered the chill factor. For the most part, the rain held off except for a few sprinkles from time to time. Along the way, we encountered some bikers who were stopped while one of their group changed a flat tire. They asked us if we had any wine we could give them — an odd question for the Camino, I thought. We stopped at a rather dismal picnic area and had some nuts and crackers for lunch. This was near the road to *Villamarco* and well beyond the half-way point of our day. In this place we saw graffiti painted on one of the benches that informed us that we were equal to Nazis!

In the small hamlet of *Reliegos*, we came upon the *Bar La Torre*, colorful inside and out. I stopped to take a picture and Greg went inside to get a Coke Light. After a second or so, he poked his head out and beckoned me inside. Every inch of every wall was covered with some type of memorabilia of The Camino.

Within another hour, we reached *Mansilla de las Mulas* and quickly found the rather non-descript hotel that would be our resting place. Our host was a rather gruff elderly woman who seemed to not care if we were there or not. She showed us to our room upstairs and then informed us that there was no Wi-Fi whatsoever in the hotel but that there was internet downstairs. This turned out to be a PC hooked up to the internet that cost 2 Euros for 5 minutes. I took a shower in the room and went downstairs to get a beer. There was a fellow Spanish pilgrim there watching a tennis match and rooting for Rafael Nadal. Greg came down and we decided to go foraging for tomorrow's food. No markets were open. In fact, no stores were open — Siesta! Back in the room, it was too early for our favorite TV game show, so we watched "Evita", starring Madonna. By now the rain had started, and the room was quite cold. I found a blanket in the armoire and huddled under it and fell asleep for a couple of hours. By the time I awoke, it was time for dinner. Down in the dining room, the same woman was serving the meal. It was then that I noticed that she smelled really bad and this made the meal less appetizing. At a nearby table were the two Irish ladies we had seen along the way several times. They were from Dublin and quite pleasant to talk to. They would be finishing their Camino in *Ponferrada*, taking a bus from there to *Santiago* and then home to Ireland. They had already walked from *Ponferrada* to *Santiago* and told us of their adventures. After they left to go upstairs, Greg and I figured that there was absolutely nothing to do in this hotel or town, so it was better just to go up to our cold room and get some sleep. We also discussed not walking to *Leon* the next day, since most of the short way was on hardscape. This was a strong recommendation in the Brierley Guide Book. I was certainly OK with this since it would give my blisters some relief. I had also seen in the guide book that there was a health clinic nearby (*Centro Salud*). This could be an opportunity to have the *"ampollas"* looked at by a professional. We decided that we would indeed take the bus to Leon in the morning and I would decide about the *Centro Salud* at that time.

Day Twenty-Three: Mansilla de las Mulas to Leon

It was just as cold in the morning, and it appeared that no heat came on at all during the night. This was certainly the worst of the hotels we had stayed at thus far. Breakfast was actually not too bad, but served by the same grumpy, smelly woman. I told Greg that I had decided to not go to the health clinic after all, since I was certain that they might tell me I had to stay off my feet for a couple of days. So, after we ate and set our bags out, we took off and found a *mercado* that had great food and snacks for the day. We headed northwest towards the bus station and soon found that we had gone several blocks too far, so we had to circle back and take a left behind a large gas station and there was the *Estacion de Autobuses*. Just as we arrived a bus was taking off, and the driver waited for us to get on. Sitting on the bus, I wondered why we had bothered to get any food because within twenty minutes we were arriving at the bus station in *Leon*. Exiting the station in *Leon*, we headed north along the *rio Bernesga* and crossed at the bridge leading to *Av. Ordono* and into the bustling downtown of the city.

It was a beautiful day and at first sight *Leon* appeared to be a nice city with perhaps the greatest degree of modernity we had seen since *Burgos*. The stores were full of shoppers on this Saturday morning as we headed in the general vicinity of our hotel. I needed some new laces for my boots since I had tied a knot in one of them and was unable to get the tight fit I wanted. We found an outfitting store just a few blocks down the street and Greg also decided he would use this opportunity to get a new hat to replace the one he had lost several days ago. I got some perfect laces and Greg found the hat he wanted after trying on several of them. The store clerk was also very helpful in giving us directions to our hotel, and he drew us a little map to help us along the way. Within a few minutes we found the *Plaza Isidoro* and our magnificent hotel nestled in this beautiful, active monastery.

Our room was not yet ready, so we left our backpacks there and walked around the area for an hour or so and had some lunch at *Hotel Boccalino* on the opposite side of the plaza behind our hotel. Truly delicious food.

After the leisurely meal, we strolled back to the hotel and sat in the lobby for a while talking with a bevy of American students from the University of North Carolina who were on a tour that consisted of biking and hiking on parts of the Camino as well as taking some history classes with the professors who were also tour guides.

Before long, our room was ready and we settled in for what we hoped would be an enjoyable couple of days in this great city. The desk clerk told us that we could leave our laundry at the front desk and they would send it out to be returned the following day. We took care of that and then decided to head out for some sightseeing at the north end of town. I wanted to make sure I saw the *Parador* Hotel which is where everyone stayed in the movie *The Way*. Within a few minutes walk, we found the *Parador*, as well as the *Iglesia San Marcos*, its attached Cloisters and museum, and the statue of the Weary Pilgrim. Plenty of opportunities for picture taking in this beautiful location, and I took full advantage of it.

Once again, I found that the Wi-Fi only worked in the lobby area, so I found a comfortable chair there and set about contacting everyone at home and posting pictures of the day's activities. I also emailed Susan and Carrie to see if they were going to be in town tomorrow. The desk clerk told me that dinner at the hotel was at 9:00 pm but that it was reservation only and the serving was already fully booked. That was OK with me since I knew that we would be hungry way before that. I then went back up into the room and found Greg sound asleep. This seemed like a good idea to me and I was soon in dreamland on my bed. Around six o'clock we woke up and got ready to go out to find a place to eat. Realizing that the same late-night hours for eating were once again prevalent as they had been in *Pamplona* and *Burgos*, we decided to go back to *Boccalino*. We headed back there across the plaza and found a table near the window so we could watch the activity of the street. After we got our food, the two German guys came in, and when they saw us it was a great reunion. They sat at their own table however, which they always did, respecting our privacy perhaps, or maybe because we had already started eating. One of them spoke fairly good English. In *Calzadilla*, I had informed him that I had lived in *Heidelberg* for 18 months a long time ago when he was just a little boy. He got a real kick out of this and started singing, "I left my heart in Heidelberg" (*Ich hab mein herz in Heidelberg verloren…"*) His name for me now was *Heidelberg*. His companion, just saluted, smiled and drank his beer. After dinner, it was back to the hotel and to bed. What a pair of deadbeats we were! Neither of us had slept well in that cold room in *Mansilla*, so we were anxious to get a comfortable night's sleep.

NOTE: From this point on, I have decided to combine the notes and recollections from both my first and second Caminos. As a reminder, Camino No. 1, from St. Jean Pied de Port to Santiago, was taken in the spring of 2013 with my good friend, Greg Sutter. Camino No. 2, from Leon to Santiago was taken in the fall of 2015 with my wife, Heather. There are many similarities, but also some big variances in the routes, distances and places we stayed on both trips.

Camino No. 1--Day Twenty-Four: A Day in Leon

Breakfast in the dining room was magnificent, just like the hotel. There was an ample buffet that had various meats and cheeses along with many kinds of fruit and good scrambled eggs. Even though we knew we were going to be in town the entire day, we still took some oranges and rolls with us — just couldn't help it, I guess. While eating we discussed the suggestion in the Brierley guide book, to consider taking the bus tomorrow to *La Virgen del Camino*, the first little town at the outskirts of *Leon*, principally for the same reasons we took the bus coming in — all industrial area with nothing but hardscape and dangerous traffic all the way.

On the way back to the room after breakfast, I asked the desk clerk where we could catch the bus. She showed me on the map where the stop was to get the right bus, and that was very helpful. Greg and I then set out to the *Plaza San Domingo* to find that bus stop so we didn't have to search in the morning. We were certainly glad we did this because the Plaza had several spokes that spread out in all directions. But we were able to find the appropriate stop and set out to do some sightseeing. We discovered that the bus stop was not far from the *Casa Botines*, a beautiful Gaudi architectural masterpiece where we hoped to encounter the statue of the man himself. Two blocks later we turned the corner and there it was!

As I contemplated this intriguing work, I remembered my week in

Barcelona about 40 years ago where I first encountered the works of Gaudi, especially the splendid *Catedral de Sagrada Familia*. At a bench at the front of the building, I sat down with the artist and reviewed his sketch pad with him.

From *Casa Botines*, it was a short walk to *Plaza Mayor* where there was a marvelous open-air market in full swing.

From here it was just a few short blocks to *Plaza Regla* and the wonderful Gothic splendor of the *Leon Cathedral*. This was one of the first cathedrals to be opened up with stained glass windows that reached to the highest points. At the top of the windows were the representations of the Holy Trinity and below them were all creation, flora and fauna. We spent approximately two hours touring the inside of this wonderful 13th century structure along with the cloisters that are adjacent.

Winding our way through the narrow streets outside the Cathedral, we arrived back at *Plaza Isadoro*, just in time to get a pizza at *Boccalino*. Why not? I checked my phone at the restaurant and saw an email from Susan indicating that they were in town, staying at a hotel near the *Plaza Mayor* and that she and Carrie would be happy to meet us for dinner later in the day. I emailed back that *Boccalino* was a great spot to eat and that they served full meals any time of the day. Susan said she was waiting to get something from her husband so they would not be able to meet us until 7. Greg and I agreed that this was a good time and so we set the time for seven. After the pizza, it was time to go back and get a nap in. Later, we ascertained that this was much needed rest on these "days off". We arrived at the restaurant just before seven and got a table to wait for our Canadians. Five minutes later they arrived, but there was an additional person: Bruce, Susan's husband had surprised her by flying into *Leon* that afternoon and taking a cab to the hotel! It was their 40th wedding anniversary, so a great surprise. We all enjoyed a great dinner and a couple of bottles of good wine. Bruce, Susan and Carrie were all going to stay in *Leon* for another day and Bruce would walk with them to *Santiago*. After dinner, we said goodbye outside the restaurant in front of the *Basilica de San Isidoro*.

Camino No. 2. Arrival in Spain and journey to Leon.

After a seemingly endless night over the *Oceano Atlantico*, the sun began to rise just under the enormous wing of the Boeing 777. It painted the clouds below with a faint rose/orange hue and served as a signal that our long flight would soon be over. Before long we were passing over *La Coruna* and headed southeast towards *Madrid*. I woke Heather up so she could see the sunrise, and she was surprised that she had slept for so long and that we would only have an hour and a half until touchdown.

We arrived in *Madrid* earlier than scheduled and then began the long process of first walking the entire length of T4 at *Barajas* to passport control, then boarding a shuttle to baggage claim. Happy to see our bag on the conveyor belt as soon as we arrived — always a relief!

After leaving baggage claim, we exited out into the main arrival portion of the terminal and made our way downstairs to the RENFE train connection area. Heather waited in a long information line while I went to a special ticketing area, showed my printed tickets to the agent, and received two passes to get us thru the turnstiles. I hailed Heather from the far end of the building and she pulled out of the line and brought the bag up. Reaching the turnstiles, a young woman saw that we seemed a bit confused, and offered to help us navigate through to the *Cercanias* train. She explained the train stops to us and promised to alert us when the *Chamartin* stop was coming up.

When we arrived at *Chamartin*, we got off the *Cercanias* and made our way up the platform steps to the main terminal. There we needed a little bit of help from Information to ascertain that our train gate would only be posted 20 minutes before "*Salida*" (departure). Since we had over ninety minutes to go, we decided to chill out and get some water and a Coke Lite and munch on some almonds that Heather had stowed away.

After a walk around the terminal, it was soon time to make our way through Gate 14 and down to the platform where we had our tickets scanned and waited for the Alsa train.

The journey to *Leon* lasted nearly three hours and we had brief stops at *Valladolid* and *Palencia* before reaching our destination. It was easy to find a taxi right outside the RENFE station, and the drive to *Hospederia Monastica Pax* was less than ten minutes. Fare was only €6.50. At the front desk we were greeted by a delightful *hospitalera*, and we checked into our room, quite relieved that we had made it safely.

After showers and unpacking, we set off for a brief walk up to *San Isadora, the Casa de Spiritualidad* and then ended up at *Restaurant Boccalino* for a Pizza Marguerite. Then back to the hotel where our fatigue finally overcame us.

Camino No. 2. Day in Leon

Upon awaking, it appeared that we had gotten the jet lag behind us. Yesterday we slept until 10 am and barely made *desayuno* in the hotel dining room. As these breakfasts go, this is a pretty good one with plenty of real black coffee and fresh, delicious fruit.

After squaring ourselves away, we ventured out into the noisy streets towards *Plaza Mayor* where I remembered seeing a farmer's market two years ago. It was empty this time around so we sat for awhile and watched some busy pigeons scavenge for crumbs. From here it was just a short walk to the Cathedral. We paid the 5€ entry fee and basked in the beauty of this remarkable Gothic achievement. The Cloisters were not open, so we exited to the plaza and crossed over to a gift shop where Heather purchased souvenirs and a Camino bracelet for herself.

I wasn't feeling that great and didn't want lunch, but Heather went into a fast food restaurant and got a *bocadilla* and a Coke which she took back to the hotel to consume. I fell asleep soon after and took my own siesta. Heather woke me up about 5:45 and said she was going to the Vesper service at the attached monastery, and I went back to sleep.

Later on we walked over to *Plaza San Isadora* and ate dinner at *Hotel Boccalino*. At the end of dinner, a weary pilgrim came over and sat down near us. We struck up a conversation with him and learned that he was from *Santa Fe, NM*. He was suffering from tendinitis in his leg and was taking four days off after busing in from *Carrion de Las Condes*. He explained how his walking buddies would catch up with him in a few days and hopefully, by then, he would be better. We wished him well and said goodnight. Back at the hotel we arrived just in time for the Pilgrim's Blessing service in the chapel and then climbed the stairs to our room to get some sleep.

Heather didn't sleep too well, and we got up today around 9:30 and had breakfast downstairs. I decided that it would be a good idea to get some extra cash for the next couple of days out in the countryside, so I ventured out to the nearest bank and used the ATM machine to get some Euros. No problems whatsoever. Heather wanted some body *crème* so I found a *perfumerie* on *Calle Ancho* and bought some *"Vasenol cacao radiante"* (Vaseline Intensive Care). During this errand I discovered that the farmer's market was in full swing in *Plaza Mayor* so I went back to the room to get Heather. We then left to see some more sights and walked all the way to *San Marcos* and the *Parador* Hotel. The *San Marcos* cathedral was completely empty, so we sat there for a while and prayed for our loved ones back home. On the way back, we stopped at the farmer's market for some fruit and then at a local *panaderia* for some bread and made our way back to *Hospederia Monastica*. On the way up the stairs Heather tripped and fell, ripping part of one of her big toe nails off. We bandaged it up and hoped for the best.

At 6:30, we attended the Vespers and then headed back to *Plaza Isidora* for dinner. Tomorrow would be our first day of walking and we were pretty excited about it.

Chapter Eleven

Leon to Rabanal

Camino No. 1 -- Day Twenty-Five: Leon to Villadangos del Paramo

Since our bus did not leave until 10:00 am, we enjoyed a leisurely breakfast and stocked up on fruit and bread once again. We got ourselves together and walked the few blocks to *Plaza San Domingo*. At the bus stop, we watched a couple of buses come by that were not the right color (they are all color-coded), while we saw the blue buses stopping at an adjacent stop across the plaza. Since that was what we were looking for we decided to go over there and see what we could find out. One blue bus stopped and let out its passengers, and I asked the driver where the bus to *La Virgen* would stop and load. He told me to stay put. We had just missed the earlier bus, but a new one would come in about *uno hora*. So, we sat down and waited. It came as promised and we got on and found a seat. The bus wound through the busy streets, crossed the river and headed west through a predominantly urban industrial section of *Leon*. The guide was right as usual. Out the windows, we could see our fellow pilgrims battling traffic and busy highway interchanges. Within 15 minutes, we were arriving in *Virgen del Camino*. A local twenty-something noticed that we were pilgrims and told us which stop to get off. We thanked him and exited the bus and walked across the street where we found the yellow arrow signs to get us back on the Camino. After crossing the busy A-66, we were once again back on the *Senda*, only this time it was alongside the much more heavily travelled N-120. We stopped in the little town of *Valverde* where we saw this interesting wood cut-out in a local garden.

In *San Miguel* we stopped for lunch at a bench along the road and were soon joined by a young girl from China. In very broken English, she told us she had just arrived in *Leon* the day before and was walking to *Santiago* by herself. Her primary reason to come to Spain was to escape her domineering father who was smothering her. She needed to get some time away and thought this would be a good place to do it. We shared some of our food with her and wished her well. Just outside of *San Miguel*, we caught up with Priscilla who was also headed to the same hotel in *Villadangos*. We spent the rest of the day walking with her and getting to know her better.

We arrived in *Villadangos del Paramo* in the late afternoon and easily found our hotel. There was a young staff in the bar/café area who greeted us cheerfully and showed us our rooms. I couldn't help but notice the contrast between this welcome and the one in *Mansilla*. Priscilla was staying in the next room. After getting settled in, I went down to the bar for a drink. There I met Nicolas, a native Austrian who was now living in Germany with his wife and two daughters. He was taking two weeks to walk from *Leon* to *Santiago* by himself. Nicolas was a delightful fellow who had travelled extensively in the USA on business. He was a software engineer. Greg soon joined us and later Priscilla came down and we all ate dinner together.

Camino No. 2 -- Day One and Day Two: Leon to Mazarife and then to Villares De Orbigo.

Two glorious, albeit physically-challenged days were now behind us. The journey to *Mazarife* was a little longer than we thought it would be. We ended up walking 15 miles and were exhausted when we finally made it. Heather was amazing. I knew she was hurting, but she never complained. *Tio Pepe Albergue* in *Mazarife* was friendly but somewhat noisy. Our room was quite small and the shower was a challenge, but we made it work. We had dinner with a French couple who were delightful, so I had a great opportunity to practice my French.

I woke up at 6 am and started rustling around the room. We were surprised to find that *desayuno* was *includo*, and even more delighted that the host made us some excellent Cafe Americano. We each had two cups and were soon on the road.

The remote country roads stretched out through seemingly endless corn fields that were lined by beautiful wildflowers, rosehip shrubs, and thickets of blackberry vines. Heather was fascinated by the wildflowers and stopped often to photograph them.

Before long we were entering *Hospital de Orbigo* and passing over the magnificent *Puente Romana*. From there it was just a short jaunt through though some active farmlands to *Villares de Orbigo* and our destination for the night, *Albergue de Villares*. This is a marvelous place with wonderful hosts and a relaxing atmosphere.

Between *Mazarife* and *Orbigo* was more flat road walking, but stillness surrounded us most of the way, and we were passed by few, if any, other pilgrims. Heather found many different flower varieties once again, so we stopped often to get some good pictures. By late morning we were arriving at the old roman bridge in *Hospital de Orbigo* and soon through the town to the outskirts amid the farmland where we would find our next resting place in *Villares de Orbigo*. On the way, Heather made an attempt to lift a hay bale with absolutely zero success. I warned her about this, but she still insisted that she should at least give it a try. After taking a wrong turn, we wound thru the town to find our *albergue* and checked in with our delightful *hospitalera*, Christine and her husband Stephan. There was time for us to wash some of our clothes and hang them out to dry on the dryers furnished by the *albergue*. We met the other guests for the night as they came straggling in. Four ladies from Finland, one from Germany and one from USA. Heather and I both took naps and showers, and fairly soon it was time for dinner. Everyone sat at a large table set up outside in the courtyard, while Christine entertained us with her "speech" that she gives to all the pilgrims as they come through, then proceeded to serve us a delicious five-course meal which she told us was "*donativo*". The dessert was a fruit cobbler served with vanilla ice cream. She called this her masterpiece.

At dinner we had great conversations with the other guests. The girl from USA turned out to be from Boston. She was suffering from bad tendinitis in one of her legs and was concerned about how far she could go from this point.

After dessert, Stephan served us all an *aperativ* from a large tray which contained many selections. After the festivities, I complemented Stephen and Christine on their artistic display of old artifacts that lined the entry to the *albergue*.

In the morning, Christine had prepared an enormous breakfast feast (also *donativo*) for us all inside in the kitchen area where she joined us to talk about walking from hereon. She had a suggestion for us to take the alternative route after *Astorga* that led to *Castrillo de las Polvazares* because it was a beautiful little village not to be missed. We thought we might try that since it wouldn't take us out of our way too much. I made sure to drop a generous offering into the *donativo* box that was at least what we would have paid for both meals at restaurants.

As we walked off, we turned right and they shouted after us and told us to turn left as they waved goodbye with big smiles on their faces. An unexpected and delightful experience. *Albergue Villares de Orbigo* is highly recommended. It is only 2.2 km from Hospital and well worth the extra little jaunt.

Camino No. 1 -- Day Twenty-Six. Villadangos to Astorga.

Greg and I got an early start. We didn't see Priscilla or Nicolas when we left right after breakfast. We did run into Nicolas however about halfway to *San Martin* and said hello. It appeared that he wanted to walk alone and we left him there. In a couple of hours, we arrived in *Hospital de Orbigo*. By now the sun had come out and it was a beautiful day. At the famous *Puente* we ran into an American couple who had just joined the Camino in *Leon*. The woman asked me to take their picture overlooking the bridge, which I did. Then she looked at the picture I took and asked me if I would take another, but this time without my thumb in the picture. It was a pretty snotty remark, the way she said it, and Greg and I would laugh at this from time to time.

As we crossed in the main part of town, we could see the jousting field on our left. It looked as if they were preparing the field for an event to come later in the month.

On the other side of the bridge, we stopped at a small park right on the Camino in the center of town and ate lunch. Just as we were wrapping up lunch, Priscilla came strolling by. She joined us and walked with us for a while. Outside of town we quickly entered a farming area where there were crops surrounding us. Ahead of me I noticed a young woman really struggling to get along. Greg thought her pack was too heavy for her. Indeed, it was, and I noticed that she was really limping badly. I went over to her and asked if she needed help. She said that she would be alright. We wished her a good day and blessed her for safe travel from this point. Before long we got to *Santibanez de Valdeiglesia*.

Priscilla left us at this point and stopped at a bar to eat and rest. We kept going and began soon to climb up some very steep hills towards *Alto Santo Torbio*. On the way up and at a flat point of the trail, we happened upon a guy riding a unicycle. Was he kidding?

It became apparent that there were more pilgrims on the trail now since many had started in Leon and were now joining us after *Hospital de Orbigo* where the two routes came together. The sun was beating down now and we were sweating getting up the mountain to the *Alto*.

At the top, we happened upon a small cantina run by an interesting guy who lived there. He had fruit and water and other snacks spread out and they were all free for the taking, but most pilgrims were leaving donations. The water was fresh and cool. Greg took a glass, but I did not. We kept on moving to the *Cruceiro de Santo Toribio* which overlooked the town of *Astorga*, still about 5k away.

At a picnic area near the Cross, we saw the American couple once again who waved to us. I told Greg I was going to take some photos of the Cross and he told me to make sure I kept my finger out of the picture. The walk down to *San Justo* was on pavement and hard on the toes, but I was glad to be going down. Before long we crossed the *rio Tuerto* and headed towards the outskirts of *Astorga*. When we got to the RR tracks, the only way over was on this strange winding green iron structure that made us laugh uncontrollably. After that it was into the city and a steep climb up a cobblestone street, through the *Puerta Sol* and into *Plaza San Francisco*. There was a statue of a traveler that greeted us there along with some locals outside a bar who welcomed us.

We continued on through three plazas, enjoying the ambiance of the city, until we finally got to *Plaza Catedral* at the north end of town where our hotel was located. We entered into the lobby area and there was the American couple who were waiting at the desk. The woman stated: "I hope you have a reservation, because the hotel is full!" I replied that we did, and she gave me a major humph. We never saw them again. *Hotel Gaudi* was a beautiful place. We found our room after locating our bags in the lobby, and took an elevator to the third floor. The room was spacious and we had plenty of room to spread out our stuff. I opened the drapes and there across the street was the beautiful *Palacio Episcopal* by Gaudi. What a view!

Greg was first in the shower. When he came out, he got dressed and headed out to find a market and get some food for tomorrow. I took my shower, got dressed and went down to the bar for a beer and to email and Facebook. While I was there, Priscilla, Paulina, and Nicolas came in and joined me. They were staying at another hotel, but knew that we were at the *Gaudi* and set out to find us.

Nicolas wanted a list of all the hotels we were staying in so he could book them up ahead of time. I went back to the room and found my vouchers for him. Soon Greg returned from shopping. We all sat in the bar for an hour or so until the dining room opened up. After getting set up at a table, we found the waiters to be terrific and very accommodating. Before long, the two Germans came in and got a separate table. They waved in our direction and were genuinely happy to see us.

Dinner was really delicious and the conversation was even better. Our topics ranged from all the cultural differences in our respective countries to politics to religion. Paulina shared that she was a unionist, belonging to the teacher's union in Switzerland. She simply could not understand what I was talking about when I explained the issues we had in California with public unions – the power they wielded and the control they exerted over the legislature. It was just something unknown to her and quite mystifying. Nicolas told us that in Germany, the government had reached an agreement with the unions to lower their wages so they could make the whole relationship work and improve the economy. Greg and I chuckled over this – thinking about how far America was from even thinking about this concept. After dessert and some aperitifs, we all said goodnight. When we got back to the room after dinner, I noticed that Greg had purchased a new shell for my backpack to replace the one I had lost several days ago. I was very touched by this and thanked him. He had also bought some fruit for the next day's sojourn.

Camino No. 2 -- Day Three: Villares de Orbigo to Astorga.

Before long we were climbing out of *Santibanez* through some dairy farms where some friendly working dogs greeted us to let us know to just keep moving. We did stop to take some pictures of the young calves in their feeding pens, while the locals kept a close eye on us. We passed *Cruz del Valle* and began heading uphill soon after with a couple of relatively challenging climbs, not as bad as I remember the last time. Perhaps I was more tired then, having started the day in *Villadangos* some 15km further east.

At the top of the plateau, before reaching *Santo Toribio* we stopped at the Cantina run by David who lives there on the land and provides refreshments *"donativo."* I spoke with him for a few minutes, telling him that I remembered meeting him two years ago. Although I suspected that he acted similarly to all repeat pilgrims, he seemed genuinely happy to see me again, and showed me all the improvements he had made over the last two years. They were significant, to say the least. On a bench nearby a young couple that we had seen near *Cruz del Valle*, had already stopped and the young man was carving a walking stick for the girl. He was Spanish and she was from Massachusetts. Heather gave the girl one of her bandanas to adorn the walking stick.

We moved on across the mesa and slightly down to *Cruceiro Santo Toribio*. From here on such a clear day we could get a beautiful view of *Astorga* and beyond that the *Montes de Leon* which we would be climbing up over the next couple of days. All Heather could do was utter: "Oy!"

At the foot of the steep path leading directly down from *Santo Toribio*, we ran into Carol from Boston and Alicia (one of the Finnish women) from the *albergue* in *Villares De Orbigo*. Carol was really suffering with her leg injury, and Alicia had stayed with her to be of whatever help she could. Carol was hoping to get some medical treatment in *Astorga*. We all told her that most likely the best thing she could do was to rest and stay off the leg. I know this was not what she wanted to hear. A hundred meters or so down the street in *San Justo* we encountered the rest of the Finnish delegation who were now getting sunburned from the day's travels. We asked Carol if we could pray for her and she enthusiastically said "yes." I told her where we were staying in *Astorga* and that she should call on us if she needed any help, and she seemed very grateful for that. At the outskirts of *San Justo*, we crossed a noisy iron bridge and headed across the cornfields bordered by the busy N-120 and warehouses and met up with the strange green monster, a winding foot-bridge that crosses the railroad tracks.

In a few moments we were climbing up the steep cobblestone street leading to *Puerta Sol* and the *Plaza San Francisco* before making our way through three or four busy plazas and then reaching our destination for the night, the *Hotel Gaudi*, located in the *Plaza Catedral*.

Our room overlooked the plaza with an unobstructed view of *Palacio Episcopal* (another magnificent Gaudi creation) and the 15th century

Catedral de St. Marta. We then got cleaned up from the day's travels, took a short nap, ate dinner in the hotel dining room and retired to get a good sleep for a long day ahead, looking forward to the climb up, up to *Rabanal*.

Camino No. 1 -- Day Twenty-Seven: Astorga to Rabanal.

After the wonderful dinner last night, we were expecting an equally good breakfast, and we were not disappointed. Since Greg had already purchased food, we didn't need to take anything from the hotel. I appreciated the plentiful coffee that was served instead of the *demitasse* that was usual. Before locating the Camino out of town, we stopped at a shop where Greg had purchased my shell. The owner was English-speaking and very welcoming. Greg bought a T-shirt with a yellow arrow and then we set out. Just up the block from our hotel was the *Cathedral Santa Marta*. It was under construction, so we couldn't get inside to see it.

As we were picking up the Camino, we both remarked that *Astorga* really appeared to be a neat town and definitely would have been a place in which we could have stayed for another day. Some towns, we were anxious to leave (*El Burgo Ranero*?), but not *Astorga*. We headed to the northwest of town and picked up the Camino through the *Puerto Obispo* and soon we were across the A-6 and back in rural Spain.

The first town we stopped at was *Murias de Rechivaldo*. Here, we ran into Priscilla while we were having a snack, and while we were chatting with her, Robert came by and told us that he was taking the detour to *Castro de Polvares* to see the classic *Maragatos* village. Then he was off, and Priscilla stayed with us for the rest of the day as we climbed up to *Santa Catalina* and *El Ganso* before reaching the heights of *Rabanal*.

Along the way, we saw several storks in the fields and noticed that they had built enormous nests on the tallest structures in town. In *El Ganso*, we ran into one of these nests.

After a long, strenuous day of significant climbs, many of which were on rocky paths, we arrived in *Rabanal*, 3,600 ft up in the mountains. *Rabanal* is a centuries-old town on a hill lined with old stone walls and filled with pristine cobblestone streets.

We stayed at *La Posada de Gaspar*, at the top end of town. Our host was jovial and welcomed us graciously. The main bar/lobby area is open to the top of the building with the rooms fanning off around this open area. We got settled in quickly, and I, as was my usual penchant, went down to the bar for a drink until dinner was served. While sitting at the bar, I heard an American woman arguing with the host about calling a baggage service to pick up her bags the following day. He did not want to call the service for her, but was willing to give her the number for her to call. She was quite obnoxious about it, but after a while he relented and made the call. Greg came down and was intent on going on one of his forays into the town to find food. I went off in the opposite direction where it was flatter (blisters really hurting) and took some pictures of the beautiful stone walls that lined the adjoining orchards.

We had left Priscilla at her hotel earlier upon arriving in *Rabanal*. She told us she would join us later for dinner at our place if she wasn't too tired. That evening we had another good dinner. Priscilla never did make it. We didn't see Nicolas either, and he must have stayed at another hotel in town. It didn't take long to get to sleep, as usual.

Camino No. 2 -- Day Four: Astorga to Rabanal.

Toast, jam, and two OK "*cafe Americanos*" served by a gruff bartender in the Hotel Gaudi bar started our morning off before we stepped out into a beautiful sunny day in *Astorga*. Within minutes we were to the outskirts of the city past *Puerto Obispo* and headed over the freeway A-6 but not before stopping at a small medieval hermitage called *Ecce Homo*. We entered the tiny chapel and received a *sello* for our *credenciales*. Soon, the city environs gave way to countryside and we made it to *Murias de Rechivaldo* within an hour. It was here that we hoped to veer off to *Castrillo de Polvazares*, but we must have missed the turn and by the time we exited *Murias*, it was too late to change directions. Besides, that would have violated one of my core Camino principals: "never go back" because it's just that much further to get to where you are going. In spite of the urging from Christine at *Alberque Villares de Orbigo*, *Castrillo* would have to wait for another trip.

Santa Catalina was next. Before we got there we met Vince and Henrietta from Australia, and of course became instant friends as we walked along for several kilometers. We stopped for a short while to rest our feet while Vince and Henrietta waited for their friends (two other couples) to catch up. At the outskirts of *Santa Catalina*, we ran into Michel and Lisa, the French couple from dinner in *Mazarife*. Since they appeared to want to walk alone, we left them and continued on along a beautiful long trek up sandy trails through magnificent countryside.

When we got to the crumbling village of *El Ganso* we stopped for some refreshments in a cafe next to the Cowboy Bar. Heather and I both had *Bocadillos con Queso*. To our surprise the sandwiches were fresh and delicious. This was to become a staple for us in the days to come along the Camino. Heather finished off her lunch with a chocolate *Helado* popsicle! Hey, you can eat these things when you are burning off so many calories along the way!

The rest of the way up to *Rabanal* was just a delightful walk, albeit a long one. At one resting point, a British chap came over to us with some fresh watermelon and sliced off a piece for us — cold and quite refreshing. He said he had picked up a bottle of wine and a chunk of watermelon in *El Ganso* and was planning on a great lunch. We could not imagine taking on that much weight to carry, but "chacon a son gout!" Heather's hip was bothering her, but she stopped often to stretch it out, and that seemed to help.

Before entering *Rabanal*, we traversed a wooded area with a steep climb, fenced on one side. The fence is strewn with crosses fashioned into it. This is an extraordinary sight, and we stopped to photograph several of them.

Reaching *Rabanal* we climbed the steep main street to our pension *La Posada de Gaspar* and settled in for the night. At dinner, we were surprised to see Vince, Henrietta and their Australian friends as well as Michel and Lisa — all of whom appeared to be staying at *Gaspar* as well.

Chapter Twelve

Rabanal to O'Cebreiro

Camino No. 1 -- Day Twenty-Eight: Rabanal to Ponferrada

We ate breakfast as soon as the dining room opened. While seated at our table we spoke with a guy we had seen from time to time on the Camino. He was in his sixties, from Switzerland, and had walked the Camino before. This was his second or third trip I believe, and he could really move at a fast pace. He was always in the next town well ahead of us and always cleaned up and beginning his evening before we even checked in to our hotel. Quite impressive. Before long, the American woman I had heard arguing with the host yesterday came into the dining room with her husband and surveyed the scene. Gesturing with her hands, she asked: "This is breakfast?" as if to say that she had expected more than this. Greg told her this was an unusually good spread, but that was not going to mollify our American princess, and she told her husband that they would just have to go someplace else to find a better meal. He looked at us and shrugged his shoulders. We felt sorry for him. We never saw them again. It was a nice, mild morning, but the sky was overcast, perhaps because we were so high in the mountains. There was no sign of Priscilla or Nicolas on the street as we took off. Soon we were climbing on narrow mountain paths that wound up and over the *Irago* Pass. Along the way were fields of beautiful wild flowers.

An hour later we had climbed to the *Cruz de Ferro* where there was a considerable crowd gathered. We waited for an opportunity and stepped forward to lay our rocks that we had brought from California at the foot of the cross. Robert was there also and offered to take our picture.

I left the stone that Heather had given me next to mine and stopped to pray for a short time. When I had finished, I came back down the hill from the cross and saw that Greg was engaged in a "serious" discussion with Robert. Greg finally got away from him and we left to head down the hill towards *Manjarin*. Here we found a rather unique *albergue* that has become legendary along the *Camino Frances*.

From *Manjarin*, there was an exceedingly steep climb down to *Acebo*. Along the way we encountered some crazy bike riders who were coming down these rocky paths at breakneck speeds that endangered all of us. They screamed for us to get out of the way, and it was really quite annoying. The climb down was hard enough, and these guys were making it hazardous.

We came down into *Acebo* and decided this was a good place to stop and eat. There we found an old wooden bench in an alley between buildings and plunked down on that to rest. At the outskirts of *Acebo*, the view opened up to the mountains that we would soon be climbing over.

This was a daunting prospect ahead of us and a little bit intimidating for me. After an hour or so, we got to *Riego de Ambros*, a tiny place that was very well kept up.

After *Riego*, there was another extremely steep climb down on a narrow path that was once again strewn with rocks and big roots.

This was slow going, but soon we noticed that there were some middle aged Germans who were seemingly undaunted by the present danger. They were nearly running down the hill, all the while laughing and having a good old time. After passing them as they stopped to rest for a bit, we could hear them behind us as they once again were on their way and coming closer to us. Greg, who was slightly ahead of me, looked back up the trail and grimaced as he stated that one of the Germans had fallen. I was not surprised to hear this. We stopped and looked back for a while, but it appeared that the others in the group were attending to their friend. Since there was more laughter, we assumed everything was OK. Before long, the group had caught up to me, and as the fallen one passed, noticed that he was bleeding from his ear. I indicated this to him, and he shrugged it off. That was the last we saw of this group.

In an hour or so, we descended into *Molinaseca*, through hills filled with wild flowers, but before entering the town, we found a bench on the east side of the river by the bridge and took our shoes off to change socks and let our feet dry out.

Greg was feeling the effects of a cold that was coming on, and I needed to get some more blister tape, so we decided to try and find a *Farmacia* in *Molinaseca* before moving on to *Ponferrada* where we would spend the night. After getting our shoes back on, we crossed the bridge into the delightful old part of town.

Greg needed to stop at a local bar to go to the bathroom, so I waited at a table outside where I struck up a conversation with a woman from Denmark who had bandages all over her feet. We shared our blister stories. She had stopped in *Leon* for a couple of days and gone to a clinic and received professional treatment. She was hurting though as she walked along and had to stop often to rest. Greg came out of the bar with a coke and sat with us for a while. We all introduced ourselves. The woman's name was Elsa. She had also run into the other woman from Denmark, Frida, that we had first met in *Hornillos*. After about ten minutes, Greg and I took off, found a local *Farmacia* and got what we needed. The road out of *Molinaseca* was a long uphill and then a long downhill on residential streets before we crossed over the *rio Boeza* and into *Ponferrada.* I suppose we were so tired by the time we reached the inner city, that we missed our turn to the right by the *Castillo de los Templarios,* and we headed downhill on *Av. Del Castillo* and wound up on the other side of *rio Sil*. Fortunately, we discovered our mistake before we went too far, and re-traced our steps back up the hill, across the river and turned left by the *Castillo*.

After walking through the *Plaza Encina*, we eventually found the *Plaza Ayuntamiento* and the *Hotel Aroi Bierzo Plaza*. We checked in and got up to our beautiful and spacious room and flopped down on our beds, exhausted.

The Wi-Fi worked in the room, but we were both too tired to even post messages and email. I was first up and into the shower only to discover that there was no hot water! I took a cold shower and dressed. Then I told Greg about the predicament and went down to the desk to complain. The desk clerk said she would send a repairman up to our room and see what was wrong. Ten minutes later, no one had come. After complaining again, we discovered that there was a problem hotel-wide with the water. We both laughed, realizing that there were probably many others out on the Camino that would have gladly taken a cold shower and would have been happy to have this beautiful room and bed to sleep in. Greg went in to get a cold shower. Later we found an Italian restaurant on the plaza and had a good meal. *Ponferrada* was a big city, and we were surprised at its modernity. We were staying in the old section of town and were distressed to see how many beautiful buildings had been ravaged with graffiti.

Camino No. 2 -- Day Five: Rabanal to Riego de Ambros.

We were refused service in the main dining room at *Posada Gaspar* and told that the area was for groups only, then directed to the bar upstairs where we found another couple eating toast and coffee, having had the same experience. We all laughed it off as just a simple oddity. I was remembering my trip two years ago in this very establishment when a young woman stepped into the dining room in the morning and said with a superior attitude: "This is breakfast??" Greg and I had both gotten such a laugh out of this that I decided that I would try and direct Heather to re-create this scenario. I coached her in the proper body language, vocal inflection and facial expression until I felt she had it down, then took a picture of her in this pose.

Behind my back, Heather could see the woman who served us the food wondering what was going on, and then of course we felt a bit embarrassed, being completely unable to explain what in the world we were doing.

We were out the door by 8:30 and headed up the stone path in the cool morning air. After about five minutes, we saw a familiar figure coming from ahead back our way. It was Alicia, our friend from Finland. She told us the other girls were up ahead and they were not sure they were going in the right direction, so she came back to check on it. I told her that we were indeed going in the right direction, since I had already been this way before. We walked together for a while and talked about Carol, who had decided to stay in *Astorga* for a couple of days. We all agreed that this was indeed the best course of action for her. We caught up with the other Finnish girls and continued along for a few hundred meters. The trail was wet from rain the night before and with normal morning dew, and as it grew steeper, we waved goodbye to our Finnish friends who were moving at a pace too fast for us. We were all certain that we would see each other again.

The climb up to *Foncebadon* is one of the most beautiful sections on the entire *Camino Frances*. Spectacular views abound, and the low-lying shrubs are speckled with gorgeous wildflowers and heather. It is truly a veritable feast for the eyes.

We stopped at a small bar in *Foncebadon* for a snack and got another stamp for our *credencials* while we were at it. Out of *Foncebadon* was a significant climb up to *Cruz de Ferro,* and while there were a good number of people there, it was not as bad as I remember last time.

Heather was overwhelmed by the scene and the importance it had to her. She did her "work", as she described it, on the far side of the cross, leaving stones and things that people had asked her to bring, as well as all the prayers from our Epiclesis family. It was a very moving time for both of us.

Before leaving *Cruz de Ferro*, Heather had an encounter with a Spanish woman who appeared to be distressed by the tourist mentality of the many people around the cross. She told Heather that it is better to come in the early morning when no one is there in order to have more time for meditation, but of course that was not possible for us. We moved on down this "highest point on the *Camino Frances*" along the well-kept path that leads down to *Manjarin* and then up once again to *Punto Alto*.

At a rest stop at the top we stopped and got a sandwich, coke and water. A kindly German man came over to Heather and gave her a tin of salve which he recommended she massage into her quad muscle. Apparently he had seen us stopped along the way and seen that I was rubbing her thigh to loosen up this muscle. She thanked him and immediately rubbed the salve in. The Germans were traveling in a group of about six, and they all began to engage us in a lively conversation. They were fascinated that we had come from so far away in California, and all expressed a desire to go there someday. One of the women told us that her 95-year old mother had made the salve from Calendulas. They told Heather to keep the tin, since they had another along with them.

We finished eating and made our way across the road and up onto the trail that led to the steep descent into *Acebo* where we stopped to stretch and get some water.

Within an hour or so we were coming into the little town of *Riego de Ambros*, our resting place for the night. We found the Pension where we were staying up across the main road and settled in to our room, tired and aching from a good up and down day. After we had showered in what was clearly the smallest shower in the world, we got dressed and headed down the hill and across the road to the only restaurant for dinner. The Pilgrim's menu was 9 Euros and the food quite good. Time to get a good sleep, and tomorrow night we would be out of the country and into the major regional city of *Ponferrada*.

Camino No. 2 -- Day Six: Riego de Ambros to Ponferrada

Our hostess at *Pension Riego de Ambros* had a delightful breakfast prepared for us on this morning of our 31st wedding anniversary. She did not charge us for the meal and wanted that to be her gift to us on this special day — just one of the many kindnesses we received throughout our long trek! We finished eating and set out down the steep hills to *Molinaseca*.

Just across the beautiful roman bridge into town, we found a great bar/cafe and had *cafe con leche* and some delicious pastries that were supplied by the owner. Then we set out along the long uphill road towards *Ponferrada*. Following the suggestion in the Brierley guidebook, we veered left towards *Campo* and took the gravel track down the hill and into the little village, eventually reaching *Los Barrios* at the outskirts of the city and climbed up to the *Castillo de los Templarios*. As we approached the city we could hear fireworks and cannons going off at a regular clip. It was soon apparent that we had arrived during a major fiesta. The streets from the castle leading into the Old Town were filled with celebrants and craft booths making passage through the crowd difficult. I could see the conflict growing on Heather's face as I know she wanted to stop at the booths and see all the artifacts and clothing on display, but was also in pain from her right quad that was really hurting. We made it to the *Hotel Aroi Bierzo Plaza* within a few minutes and checked in. Our room had a window looking out over the main *Plaza Ayuntamiento* that was now all set up with a huge stage, tents and chairs.

We took showers and stretched out to relax for the rest of the day. While Heather was resting up, I ventured down to the restaurant and ordered *Pimientos Padron* and a cheese plate with bread and brought that to the room. It was probably the best lunch meal we had during our entire trip.

Later, I went back downstairs and walked to the castle to get some more pictures of this amazingly well-preserved structure. It was closed to entry for the day, but I enjoyed just looking at it.

The festival was heating up by now, and I managed to get a great video of the procession that closed the religious portion. When I returned to the room, a sound check was underway in the plaza that indicated there was definitely going to be some sort of concert before too long, so I went down to the main desk at the lobby and asked if it would be possible for them to change our room to one that was toward the back of the hotel and not on the plaza. I told them I loved our room, but it was just not going to work for us because we needed to get our sleep. They were very understanding of us two weary pilgrims and happily gave us a new room, after apologizing for the inconvenience. We moved all our stuff down the hall and set up in our new room. At 7:30, we walked to an Italian restaurant just down the block from the hotel and had a great meal while we watched all the locals come into the plaza for the concert that was just beginning with a hypnotist and magician. At the corner of the plaza near our restaurant, there was a steep staircase leading to the lower part of the city that was lined with graffiti. It made an interesting picture.

We both got Magnum chocolate *helado* bars and walked around the plaza and back to the room where within minutes we were both asleep.

Camino No. 1 -- Day Twenty-Nine: Ponferrada to Villafranca del Bierzo.

The following morning, we got up and had a great breakfast in the lower level of the hotel and set out on the plaza to find the Camino. Right in front of the hotel we ran into the Irish ladies from Dublin, who were finished walking and would take a bus from here to *Santiago*. Once again, they told us what a wonderful walk was ahead of us in *Galicia*, through all the farms and hills. I asked them if I could pray for them in the Cathedral, and they said to pray for "good intentions". Soon after they left, Greg came down from the room, and we ran into the other Irish couple that we had met along the way. The woman's sister had joined them a day or so ago and they were getting ready to head out of town also.

After some congenial chatting, we all took off together and found the Camino just a couple of blocks from the plaza. The Irish folks stopped shortly to adjust their gear and Greg and I kept on going, across the river and headed towards the outskirts of town to the west. Soon we were across the busy N-VI and into *Columbrianos*, another curious mixture of the old and new. From here we kept moving through the rural areas of *Fuentes Nuevas* and *Camponaraya* before reaching *Cacabelos* where we stopped for lunch.

We were now deep into another wine grape area known as The *Bierzo*. The vineyards stretched out for miles, just as they had in *Rioja* and *Navarre*. While we were airing out our feet at lunch, the Irish trio came by and said hello. They were stopping in *Pieros* for the night. We finished eating and took the long downhill road into *Cacabelos* and walked through the bustling town. After crossing the *ria Cua*, the road turned sharply uphill. After *Pieros*, the trail split, and Greg and I took the seemingly more scenic route northwest. This led us through some hilly country and occasionally steep uphills, but the views were definitely worth it.

It was slow going for the most part. Finally, we hit the high point of the day and began descending into *Villafranca del Bierzo*. As we came into town, there was a rather large *alberque* down on our right just before we got to *Iglesia de Santiago*. Outside the church, a man was selling fresh cherries, and Greg stopped to buy some. We took *Calle Santiago* into town past the *Castillo de los Marqueses* and climbed down the steep steps to the center of the city. From here we found our way across the *rio Burba* and located the *Casa Mendez* shortly after that.

In the lobby were two German girls we had passed continually along the way, and they were also checking in. We got the Wi-Fi code and carried our bags up to our room. Greg was not feeling well, and he now had a full-blown cold with lots of sneezing and congestion. He had been taking the medicine that he got in *Molinaseca*, but it didn't seem to be helping very much. There were no laundry facilities in the hotel, so Greg washed a lot of his stuff in the shower and tried to find places to hang everything on doors and also on chairs on the balcony. The cherries were another issue for him since he had no way of washing them or getting them dry after washing. He wound up washing them in the bathroom sink and then laying them out on a towel on the table on the balcony. More trouble than they were worth I thought. The Wi-Fi only worked downstairs near the front desk, so I took my shower and went downstairs and sat on a cold granite slab and emailed Heather and posted some pictures of the day. After that I tried to get a nap in the room, but the coughing and nose blowing was making that impossible. Greg had told Marianne that he had the flu, but there was no apparent fever, and I think he just had a bad cold. I tried to talk him out of walking the next day and for him just to take a bus to *O'Cebriero*, but he was having none of that. Tomorrow would be the big climb up the mountain, and it was sure to be quite strenuous. We decided to take the practical route that would lead us along the river road through *Pereje* to *Trabadelo*, because we knew that the climb from *Herrerias* on would be intense. Later, we had a great dinner in the hotel dining room and got to bed early.

Camino No. 2 Day Seven: Ponferrada to Villafranca del Bierzo.

At breakfast in the basement of the hotel, we met two women from Montana who had walked all the way from *Rabanal* the day before, a distance that Greg and I had done in 2013. We compared notes and bid them farewell as we went back to the room and readied for the long journey to *Villafranca*.

Wandering back through the Old City to *Plaza Encina*, we found the Camino down *Calle Randero* and were soon across the Iron Bridge. We opted to take the alternative route through *Parque de la Concordia* along the *rio Sil* and followed that until we were up out of the city and nearly into *Compostilla*. Walking through the grounds of the *Iglesia Santa Maria*, we were soon out to the suburbs of *Compostilla*. Here we stopped at a bar for *cafe con leche* and to use the restrooms. Then it was just a short jaunt to *Fuente Nuevas*. As we wound our way through the long village, we could consistently smell the distinct aroma of marijuana. We couldn't tell if it was coming from the houses or if someone was smoking weed as they were walking along.

Mystery never solved. At the back end of a small chapel, we were both caught by some exquisite iron work on a door.

All during this early part of the day, the sky was quite threatening and we were certain a storm was imminent. Only a few sprinkles to this point, however.

About 2.5 km later we were entering the town of *Camponaraya*. At the outskirts we saw a local citizen roasting peppers on a grill outside a run-down shack. Near the center of town, we sat to rest at a small park. A local woman came up to us and wished us *Buen Camino* and asked us something in Spanish that we couldn't understand. A fellow pilgrim seated nearby told us that the woman was indicating that inside an adjacent church we could get our *credencials* stamped. We told the woman we now understood, and she seemed quite happy about it. Sure enough, after we got up to leave, we saw the woman set up at the top of the steps leading to the church at a table. We gave a donation, signed the guestbook, and received the *sello* from the woman. The fellow pilgrim that helped us understand had just stopped there before us, and I noticed that she and a companion were from Italy. As is so often the case, we kept seeing them throughout the remainder of the day. Before leaving the central part of the town, we stopped at another bar and got a Coke Zero for Heather and coffee for me. Feeling refreshed, we proceeded to the end of town and crossed through the roundabout and past a bodega onto a trail that led up out of town and across the busy A-6. Almost immediately we were once again out into the countryside that was thick with vineyards and found ourselves in the midst of grape harvesting. It was at this point that the rain decided to come down in a big way, and we had to poncho up for the first time on our trip.

As we moved down through the vineyards and into a stand of eucalyptus trees, the rain let up a little and Heather removed her poncho. I kept mine on because I knew it was just a matter of time before I would need to use it again. Five km later we were entering *Cacabelos*. We kept moving, enjoying a brief respite from the rain. At the far end of town, we encountered a house that had a river running through it. Here was also located the old *municipal alberque*.

Heather was now showing signs of the right thigh strain and needed to rest often. We took every opportunity to find a comfortable sitting place where she could stretch and re-gain some strength. One of these resting spots was directly across from an interesting bar on the other side of the road.

After we passed the little village of *Pieros*, we had to choose which option to take: (1) to the east and longer through the countryside, or (2) follow the road for the shorter route. Due to Heather's condition, we decided to choose the shorter one. This led us up over the hill where we stayed on the N-120. For the most part we had good passage on the road, but there were some challenging moments when we had perhaps one foot of room to walk between the guideline and the barrier. Lots of tractors pulling carts full of grapes passed us before we got to the village of *Camino* and turned right off the road to follow the dirt track up to where it would join the alternate route. Interesting sculptures along the way here.

By now the sun had come out, but Heather's pain had grown worse. At one point she stopped midway up a hill and said she couldn't go on. It was at this point that I took her back pack and told her to hold her trekking poles out in front of her. With both packs on me, I grabbed her poles and pulled her up the hill, much like a horse would, I suppose. At the top of the long hill, we rested for awhile, and she seemed to regain her energy. By now, the uphill climbing was over and we soon joined the other Camino trail. I knew it was not long to *Villafranca* from here and encouraged Heather to stay with it. She gritted her teeth and kept on moving. What great courage, to walk through pain such as this. Within minutes we were coming into *Villafranca* and on our left was the beautiful Romanesque Church of *Santiago*, built in the 12th century with its *Puerta del Perdon* (Door of Forgiveness).

The challenge we now faced was traversing the steep hill down into the town center. I took what I thought was a shortcut to lead us through town to our hotel, but found that we and routed ourselves to the *Plaza Mayor*. While there, I decided to stop at an ATM and get some cash. I tried three different banks, and my debit card would not work at any of them. This caused great concern for me, because I knew I would need the cash going into the mountains. I decided that I would call the bank when it opened in California after I got settled into the hotel. After a few moments, we corrected our path and found the little bridge that led over the *rio Burba* and located the hotel, *Casa Mendez*. At the main desk was a familiar face that I recognized from two years ago. After we checked in, we got a drink and sat outside on comfortable sofas with a small plate of potato chips. I looked at my Fitbit tracker and it indicated that we had walked 17.9 miles that day and over 40,000 steps. A new record! The Wi-Fi was not working well and we had difficulty staying connected. Later, in the room, I called my bank in California and got through to Customer Service. After checking the records, they indicated that the ATM was trying to draw the funds out of my savings account, which I had drained out and put into my checking account. They switched back $500 into the savings account in case that happened again. I thought I would go back to *Plaza Mayor* and try again, but it was a 40-minute round trip walk to get there, and I was just too tired to do it. Fortunately, I had some remaining Euros to pay for the hotel and dinner that evening, but I really needed to get some cash from that point on. I was confident that there would be some ATMs in some of the towns the following day.

We took a brief nap after showers and went down to the dining room at 7:30. No one had told us that we needed to make a reservation, and the waitress seemed a little flustered that we just showed up. They did make room for us, however and we ordered our meal. Heather ordered trout (*Trucha*) for her Segundo and received a plate with two small trout with the heads and tails still attached. She was horrified and did the best she could to eat it, but was a challenge. I had a delicious pork dish with the omnipresent potatoes of course. Our dessert was a great ice cream cake that almost wiped away the memory of the trout staring up at Heather. At the dinner table, we got a good connection through Heather's phone and she posted some pics to Facebook. Tomorrow, we would start heading up the mountain towards *O'Cebreiro*.

Camino No. 1 -- Day Thirty: Villafranca del Bierzo to O'Cebreiro.

In the hotel dining room, we met some fellow pilgrims from Mexico whom we saw from time to time on the Camino. We got an early start. Neither Greg nor I had slept well, largely due to Greg's cold issues. He felt awful about it, but there was nothing either of us could do except just try to get through it. I was thinking that it would just be a matter of time before I came down with whatever he had. He was still intent on walking, and seemed to think that as the day went on he would rally. We crossed the river and made our way under the N-IV and found the river trail before long as we climbed up out of *Villafranca*. It was cool, but it looked as if it was going to be a beautiful day. The path along the river was close to the road, but shielded by a thick concrete barrier that helped with the sound and gave us a feeling of relative safety. In a couple of hours, we got to *Trabedelo*, a long town on a hill. When we arrived, we found a *mercado* and Greg bought some nuts to eat. We stopped when we arrived in *La Portela de Valcarce* where there was another good *mercado*. Here I bought a big loaf of fresh bread, and we packed up and got back on the Camino. In *Ambasmestas*, we ran into a guy named Tom who was originally from NYC and had retired and moved to Ashville. Strangely enough, he knew the woman we had met earlier in *Sahagun*, and it turned out that they belonged to the same walking club back home. He walked with us for a while until we got to *Vega de Valcarce* where we decided to stop for lunch. He kept moving on and was going as far as *La Faba* tonight. Greg and I had our bread and some fruit that we had taken from the hotel.

Just before *Ruitelan*, there was a small rest stop in a rather nondescript picnic area. Greg was stopped there to fix one of his shoes and check on a toe blister. I kept on going and headed up the hill and then down and across a stone bridge over a small stream and into the town of *Herrerias*. As I wound through the town, I saw a young woman that I had seen quite often before *Burgos*. There she was sitting at a table outside a café. I nodded and kept moving. At the bridge at the north side of town, she caught up to me and passed me and nimbly moved up a very steep hill. I stopped at the bridge to catch my breath, and Greg was just coming around the corner. We then headed up the hill to the left, and this was the start of it.

Within five minutes, Greg was out of sight, and I kept trudging up the hill. After a half hour, the trail turned to the left and narrowed through a beautiful sylvan setting.

Then, just past a babbling brook, it took a steep turn uphill that was still muddy from rain days earlier. It took me every bit of one-half hour just to go maybe one hundred yards up.

Around a bend near the top, the young girl I had seen earlier had stopped. I stopped too, and we struck up a conversation. She was suffering from a bad cold and said she had a fever. She thought she could make it to *La Faba* where she would spend the night. She told me she was from Australia, but was originally from Iraq, a Kurd, whose entire family had to escape the country during the evil regime of Saddam Hussein. Australia gave them sanctuary, and she actually grew up there since she was a young girl at the time. When she found out that I was American, she thanked me for freeing her country from Saddam. She was twenty-four years old, and she told me that when her family went to Australia, they had to give up their way of life. They had no choice in the matter. It was leave or die. Now that she had come to Spain to make this pilgrimage, she could joyfully say that it was her choice to come. I told her how brave she and her family were and said goodbye, hoping to see her again along the way.

At the top of this steep hill was *La Faba*, and when I reached the water fountain, Greg was waiting there. He was unsure whether or not to fill his bottle there because the fountain looked pretty bad. There were no typical potable water signs. Two other pilgrims went inside to the adjoining bar and asked the owner if it was OK to drink from the fountain. They came out and signaled thumbs up. Greg filled up and soon we were on the way up again. Once more, he got way ahead of me and I lost sight of him. For almost all the rest of the day, I was alone most of the time, although I did stop briefly at *Laguna de*

Castilla and rested at a café wall before leaving to climb back up. After Laguna, the vistas became spectacular.

I did meet one Italian bicycle rider who told me that this was the last big mountain to go over: "Once you get over it, you can smell the sea!" he said. "Until then, just drink in the beauty!" He was right. Just after that encounter I reached the provincial line and crossed over into Galicia. Graffiti had marred the sign.

Another hour of climbing at approximately 1mph finally brought me around the final bend and onto the trail that led into *O'Cebreiro*.

This charming, cobblestone village at the very top of the mountain, has a unique look all to itself. I was unable to find the hotel at first, but after five minutes of walking around I finally found it and there was Greg coming down the steps at the front of the place. He took me up to our room and I got everything unloaded. The room was tiny, but that didn't seem to matter. I took a hot shower and we went down to the bar and had dinner. Greg seemed no worse for the wear with his cold. As for me, I was exhausted, but elated that the big climb that I had dreaded was finally over. Lying in bed later, a bed that was horribly uncomfortable, I thought back to the day's accomplishments. There were times when I had thoughts that I might die on this mountain, but if so, it was a beautiful place to die.

Camino No. 2 -- Day Eight: Villafranca del Bierzo to Las Herrerias.

Toast and coffee in the dining room started out what appeared to be a beautiful morning at the foot of the mountains. We stepped out the door and turned left and were immediately on the Camino opting to take the *Pereje* route along the N-VI and following the river. We felt this choice would be the easiest on Heather's right leg and hip, and we were attempting to prevent any further injury. She felt great as the morning walk began. After a slight climb out of town, the road soon leveled out and was quite manageable for her. At this point we could look back to *Villafranca* and see where we had spent the night.

After an hour or so we stopped at a rest area in the sunshine that was now beginning to spill over the hills in the east.

We stopped again to rest in *Pereje* at the top of the long street that is called *Camino Santiago* where Heather entered a small *mercado* and tried to obtain some Ibuprofen along with some nuts and a Coke Zero. She was told by the gruff shopkeeper that the sodas were not cold so we just left the place without buying anything. Up the road about 3.5 km was a pleasant turn off into the woods before reaching *Trabadelo*. This was a nice respite from the constant noise of the busy road. We were also joined here by the pilgrims who had taken the *Pradela* Route earlier in the day, so the Camino got a little more crowded.

At *La Portela*, we stopped at a truck stop/restaurant and purchased some fresh cheese and bread, then sat outside and ate that and some cashews we had brought from home. We didn't finish all the cheese, so we gave what was left to a young pilgrim who was just stopping by, and we got up to continue on. After 1.5 km, I started to feel some nausea and was certain I was going to throw up. In *Ambasmestas*, we found a bench to sit down on for a bit. I drank some water and tried to regain my equilibrium. In a few moments I could feel the nausea subside to some degree and decided to give walking a go once again.
After a few hundred meters, I was back to normal. Whew! We were thinking that the cashews might have been rancid.

From this point, we followed along the river through a series of delightful villages with lovely country homes painted in bright colors. It was a magnificent day. There were wildflowers galore along with personal and communal gardens that were still thriving at this time of year. In *Vega de Valcarce*, we ran into our Australian friends Vince and Henrietta who were staying at a *pension* there for the night. Henrietta had been injured and had taken a taxi for a couple of days, but she was hoping to walk the next day. They said with confidence that they would see us tomorrow at the top of the mountain. We said goodbye and headed towards *Ruitelan*. In *Ruitelan*, we were able to stop at an ATM and get some Euros and right next door was a *Farmacia* so Heather could get some Ibuprofen and *Compeed* for her *Ampollas* (blisters).

After *Ruitelan*, the trail led back to the main road, and we had a steady, but relatively short, climb until we reached the outskirts of *Las Herrerias*. Our pension was just off the road to the left, and it was a special place. We settled in here around 1:00 pm. Heather strung up a clothesline in our room and washed out some of our things. Some we put out on our balcony in the sunshine. After a shower, I went downstairs, and had a large beer while I logged on to the Internet through the Wi-Fi connection that would not work in the room. After a while, Heather came downstairs, and we sat in the warm sunshine while several more guests checked in. At 7:30 we had a wonderful dinner in the dining room and retired for the night.

Chapter Thirteen
O'Cebreiro to Sarria

Camino No. 1 -- Day Thirty-One: O'Cebreiro to Triacastella.

Outside, the town was bustling early. There were several tour buses with engines idling for their tourists to finish final packing, get pictures taken, and board up. We thought we were getting an early start, but there were several pilgrims already underway. We moved out to the main road and started heading downhill along the side until we got to the town of Linares. While on the road, we ran into Tom who had stayed the night in *La Faba*. It was good to see him, and he walked with me for the rest of the day. Greg got out ahead of us after *Alto San Roque* where we saw an enormous statue of *The Pilgrim*.

Now, we had read about it in the guide book, and heard about it along the way, that the Camino became much more crowded from this point on and especially from *Sarria* on in. This was becoming quickly apparent. At the statue, everyone wanted to have their picture taken there, and it took forever to find a moment when no one else was in the picture. This was a little annoying, and it reminded me of the situation at the *Cruz de Ferro* several days earlier. I did the best I could. Tom and I set out down the hill to *Hospital de la Condesa* and followed the main road for a while until it veered off to the right onto a trail through the woods and fields.

At a road that head down to the north, we notice two female pilgrims ahead of us that had missed the trail to the left. We shouted at them, and they turned around and came back. They were Italians and were very thankful that we had stopped them from getting too far afield.

From here there was a steep climb up to the *Alto do Poio*. At the top is an *alberque* where a lot of pilgrims and tourists were gathered outside. One of them was Greg, who was at a table drinking a coke and fixing a blister. Tom and I decided to keep on moving and told Greg we would see him later. Tom shared a bit about his life. He was a retired IT guy from Staten Island, who worked on Wall Street in a very high-stress job. He and his wife had two grown girls who were living in various parts of the world. One daughter lived in Paris, and the other lived in Colorado, I believe. He decided to take this trip by himself, because he wanted to find out who he really was. Along the way, he found out how much he missed his wife and loved her. His daughters were going to join him in *Sarria* and walk the rest of the way with him. He was very much looking forward to this.

We stopped in *Fonfria* at a small bar/café and bought some food to eat at a table outside. About ten minutes later, Greg came by and joined us. He got a big *bocadilla* from inside. Tom had some food in his pack which he supplemented with a turkey sandwich that he bought in the bar. Greg wanted to stay for a while, but Tom and I decided to leave and move on. The walk from here was delightful and Tom and I had a great conversation along the way. Eventually, we got to some huge Chestnut trees that must have been there for hundreds of years.

We took some pictures there and kept on until we got to *Triacastela*. We stopped at the first bar in town and Tom bought drinks for us. I sat nursing my beer and Tom left to find an *alberque* at which to stay for the night. We said goodbye and realized that since he was staying an extra night in *Sarria* with his daughters, that we would most likely not see each other again. Such is the way of the Camino.

I sat at the table outside the bar for about ten more minutes and Greg finally came by. He ordered a Coke Light and soon we were heading down the street to the far end of town and found the *Casa David*. The owner was a jovial sort who led us around back to our room that was on the lower level and had an entrance via a large patio that also adjoined a back yard that had a beautiful view of the surrounding hills. He told us that if we got our laundry together and gave it to the maid, she would wash it in the hotel washer and give it back to us so we could hang it out to dry in the backyard. It was only about 3 pm and we still had a lot of sunshine left in the day, so we thought this was a great idea. We got settled in the room and assembled our laundry. After showers, I got the laundry out to the housemaid and gave her 5 Euros. She took care of the rest. About a half hour later, she knocked on the door while Greg was asleep, and I went outside to find our laundry in a neat little pile in a plastic bucket. Moving around the side of the patio, I found a basket of plastic clothespins and hung up all our stuff on the more than ten clotheslines available in the yard.

Five minutes later, a fellow woman pilgrim showed up and hung up her clothes also. She and her companion were from Canada and had just joined the Camino the day before in *O'Cebreiro*. She picked my brain about all sorts of things for the next 30 minutes. I was happy to share our experiences. This was a common courtesy that we all gave to each other along the way.

I tried to nap also, but was unable to do so. By seven, we were on our way to the middle of town to get some dinner. We saw the Canadian women at an outside table and said hello. Inside the restaurant we saw the fellow from Switzerland that we had met in *Rabanal*. He was already finished with his meal and was soon out of the restaurant. He was staying at our hotel, as it turned out. There really isn't much to do in *Triacastela*, except to sit in a bar and drink, so we just went back to the room and soon were asleep.

Camino No. 2 -- Day Nine: Las Herrerias to Fonfria

Another magnificent breakfast featuring fresh-squeezed orange juice provided the impetus for a strong start to begin the climb to *O'Cebreiro*. The early morning chill stayed with us until we were nearly out of *Las Herrerias* as some bovine friends bid us farewell with their clanging bells. Soon we were across the stream and headed up the road and reaching the turning off point. Bikes to the right and hikers to the left. Here there was a nice walk through the woods for about 500 meters until the real uphill began near a *donativo* where we found the host gathering fire-wood "for the cold weather", she said.

As we headed up this steep, rocky trail, I remembered the spot from two years ago. Then, it was wet and slippery from previous rain although the day was as bright and sunny as it was now. It was on this trail that I had met a young woman from Australia who was sick from the flu at the time. She told me that she was originally from Iraq, a Kurd, and forced to emigrate as a small child with her family to Australia as a refuge from Saddam's brutal regime. Once again, I began to marvel at how strong memories would flood back from re-visiting familiar places. The climb up was not as strenuous this time, most likely because it was early in the day, or maybe, could it be that I was just in better shape? Probably a combination of both.

We stopped at a crowded bar in *La Faba*, and Heather waited in line at the restroom while I waited in a long line to order some coffee and a Coke Zero. After she came out, we decided the wait for the food was too long and made the decision to move on and stop a bit further up. During this section we ran into Vince from Australia, and shortly behind him was his wife Henrietta and one of the other Australian women. It was great to see Henrietta walking again, and her two days of rest seemed to be paying off. We chatted for a while and then split off. From here on up, the views were magnificent, and the weather could not have been more conducive for hiking in the mountains!

Many pilgrims were stopping to take photos, and it seemed that everyone expressed the opinion that the camera just could not capture the magnificence of what was before us. When we reached *Laguna de Castilla*, we stopped and ate some fruit and health bars that we carried with us while sitting on a wall in the center of the tiny village. Then it was back up the steep trail for another half hour or so until eventually reaching *O'Cebreiro*.

Walking through the village, we found *Casa Carolo*, where I had stayed last trip, and Heather went inside and got a beer and a Coke Zero and we sat outside in the bright sunshine and enjoyed our refreshments.

Knowing we had a way to go before reaching *Fonfria*, we set out down the hill wishing that we could have spent more time enjoying *O'Cebreiro*. We stayed on the main road until reaching *Linares* and passed the ancient church of *San Esteban* with its colorful cemetery.

Then we were soon across the road and up a dirt track that led us to *Alto San Roque* to see the huge statue of the medieval pilgrim holding his hat against the wind.

By the time we got to *Hospital de la Condesa*, Heather was starting to hurt again, severe thigh pain, so we had to stop often for her to rest and stretch. The countryside had some gorgeous views from here, and we were able to capture some intriguing sights along the way.

We walked down the road to the right and out and up to a track through the woods that led to the little town of *Padornelo* with the old hermitage of *San Oxan*.

Then there was a steep, rocky climb up to *Alto do Poio* which I had forgotten completely about from last trip. This section was extremely difficult for Heather to navigate with her injury, so we had to take it really slow. At the top of the hill was *Albergue del Puerto*. I think we both silently wished we could have just stopped there for the night, as some other pilgrims were doing. I asked Heather if she wanted to stop for at least a coke, but she insisted that she wanted to keep going to get to where we were going. At least the next 4 km were on a basically flat trail that ran parallel to the main road. But when you are tired and in pain, it seems like forever to go this relatively short distance. A passing Dutch pilgrim thought that it was only a kilometer or so ahead as she blasted past us. At just about the end of our rope, we came around a hedgerow, and there, just a hundred or so meters ahead, was *Fonfria*. A very welcome sight, to say the least. *Albergue A Reboliera* was on our left as we entered town, and we quickly checked in with the friendly staff and got settled in our spot with showers and some minimal washing of socks and bandanas.

Dinner was at 7:30 down the hill in a Yurt-like structure. For an hour or so, we enjoyed a communal meal with about 40 guests. Near us at our section of the enormous table was a French couple, two Australians and a couple from Iceland. The conversation was lively and the food quite good. Especially delicious was the *Tarta de Santiago* for dessert. After dinner we hobbled up the hill and hit the sack for a well-needed sleep.

Camino No. 1 -- Day Thirty-Two: Triacastella to Sarria.

Breakfast was served in the bar at the front of *Casa David*. We ate at a small counter at the side since all the tables were occupied. Our Swiss pilgrim was also up ahead of us as usual and finishing his breakfast. After eating, Greg and I went back to the room to get our stuff and do our daily devotions. At the end of town, the Camino split into two directions, and we went to the left and followed the road and the signs to *Sarria*. After a mile or so, I began to think we might be on the wrong track since we were now seeing signs to *Samos*. I stopped to check my guide and after confirming we had taken the wrong direction, I hurried to catch up to Greg and inform him. At this point, we felt that we had gone too far to turn back, since that would probably mean going even further in the end. We decided to stay on the route and go through *Samos*. I calculated that this would ultimately take us about 4 miles more than the other direction, but if we had gone back, not only would we be losing time, we would not gain much mileage. It was an overcast day up to this point with the rain threatening. We walked for a couple of miles along the *rio Oribio* which was on our left and down a steep chasm. Eventually we crossed over the LU-633 and headed in a westerly direction up to *Capela Freituxe*. This was followed by another steep climb to *San Martino* before going down through a tunnel under the LU-633 once again and the track into *Samos*. As we came across the ridge overlooking the town, we could see the old monastery in the distance. There was a steep downhill going into *Samos*, and there were two young Spanish couples ahead of us who appeared to be coming from church. As we neared the center of town we saw a bench outside a *mercado*, and thought this might be a good place to rest and eat lunch.

Greg and I took turns going into the *mercado* and shopping for things. I bought some fresh-baked bread and some M&Ms. After eating, we started packing up when suddenly, Nicolas came down the street! It was great to see him. He gave us an update on Priscilla who he had seen a day or so ago, and he said she was doing fine. After chatting for a while, Nicolas set out to find a restaurant to get some hot soup. We said goodbye and hoped to see him down the road. *Samos* was a delightful town, and Greg and I both remarked that we were glad we took this route so we could see it. Near the outskirts of town, I saw an interesting pilgrim statue in a little park along the river dedicated to *Peregrinos*.

We walked along the river for a while after leaving the town until the yellow arrow beckoned us up a trail to the right across the busy road. From here, we climbed up a steep hill into a wooded path that led to the little village of *Pascais*. We were up along a ridge now that looked down onto the same *rio Oribio* we had been following for some time.

The river had taken a sharp turn to the north and so had we as we were now headed in the direction that would lead us to eventually join up with the other Camino route. The rain was holding off, save for a few sprinkles here and there. For the most part, we were fairly sheltered by the woods. This was becoming a really good walk. We walked through some beautiful farmland and some small villages. One bridge I crossed over in *Viega* had a little angel nestled in a protective shelter who guarded the bridge, I think.

An hour or so later, we passed through the little town of *Perros* and joined up with the other Camino trail. We noticed immediately how crowded the Camino was at this point. Again, another reason to be grateful that we had decided to take this peaceful walk through the *Samos* region.

The main trail led us west into the outskirts of *Sarria*, and there was a long walk through a residential section on the *rua do Peregrino* until we reached the *Hotel Alphonso IX*. This was truly a luxurious hotel. In the lobby, as we were checking in, we met an American couple from Ohio who were just joining the Camino to walk to *Santiago*.

The desk clerk informed us that dinner in the formal dining room was not until 9:00 pm, but that we could eat in the Cafeteria with the same menu at 7:00. That was not a hard decision for us. Up in the room we stretched out in the most spacious room we had had up to this point and enjoyed the luxury of a great shower in a truly spectacular bath. I removed my blister bandages to check out how I was doing, and Greg was aghast at how big the blisters were. 40 minutes later I had dressed the *"ampollas"* with new bandages and tape that would last for another couple of days at least, I hoped. Later we went down to the cafeteria and had a beer to wait for dinner hour. The place was filling up fast and we got a table and ordered the specialty of the house which was steak served raw at the table for us to cook on a table-top grill. While we were eating, we calculated that we had actually walked 18 miles this day. Easy to get to sleep after this.

Camino No. 2 -- Day Ten: Fonfria to Samos

Before the steep downhills to *Triacastella*, we were treated to beautiful mountain top views at approximately 4,200 feet altitude. The lush vegetation opened up before us on both sides along nearly immaculate wide trails. I remembered this section of the trip from two years ago as one of the most enjoyable days of walking. This time was no different in that regard. We slowed our pace considerably after *Biduedo* when the path became somewhat precarious. Heather was trying to keep her right quad muscle from acting up, and was taking it easy. Near the medieval villages of *Villoval* and *Pasantes*, we came across a familiar sight, a huge chestnut tree that is, I am sure, ancient.

Winding through the old villages, we eventually came into *Triacastella*, and we found *Casa David* where Greg and I had stayed last trip. We stopped here for some Coke and coffee, and I was surprised to find our old host from before. He was quite friendly and bid us *buen Camino* after we had eaten a delicious *bocadilla con queso*. From *Casa David*, we found a *supermercado* to get some supplies and then headed back out of town, down the road into the *Galician* forest and towards *Samos*.

After *San Cristobo*, we had to poncho up because the rain was starting. Behind us we heard two women chattering, and soon we realized it was the two South African ladies we had met in *Las Herrerias*. We stopped to say hello, and they were soon past us, although we kept passing each other from time to time all the way to *Samos*. By 2pm or so, we had caught sight of the old monastery and were descending into the town. We stopped at a small store on the outskirts of town and asked directions to our hotel. Within minutes we were crossing the intricate bridge over the river and winding through the streets past the monastery to *Domus Itinerus*, our *pension* for the night.

When we entered the lobby of the hotel, we had to ring the bell for the host who informed me through a translation program on his PC that the water was not working in *Domus Itinerus*, and since he had no way of reaching me, he took the liberty of booking another hotel just across the street. So we stayed at *Hotel Victoria* which had a pleasant outdoor cafe set up. The room was small and a bit dank, but fine for sleeping. We ate dinner in the bar downtown, and after the meal, we took a brief stroll through this section of town around the monastery grounds.

In the morning I took our bag back across the street to the *Domus Itinerus* lobby since *JacoTrans* would be coming there to get it, and then headed back to our hotel where Heather and I ate toast, coffee, etc. before setting forth to our next destination.

Camino No. 2 -- Day Eleven: Samos to Sarria

The Camino trail picked up just a block from *Hotel Victoria* and wound around the far side of the monastery. As we headed west out of town, we passed a bar and, to our delight, were greeted by Thiago, our friend from Brazil. We were happy to see him and find that he was still walking, albeit with some difficulty. We snapped a picture with him and traded email addresses. Since he was still eating breakfast, we left him there with the hope of seeing him sometime down the road.

Before long, the rain started coming down and we had to get out our ponchos as we made our way on the roadside path along the river. During this stretch, we passed a statue of an old pilgrim who I remembered well from my last trip.

As we headed northwest to meet up with the standard route to *Sarria* from *Triacastela* via *San Xil*, we passed through several small hamlets and farms for 8 km or more, all dotted with old stone structures and inhabited with local livestock. One old roman bridge was guarded by a stone angel, another fond memory from 2013.

Just after *Perros* we spotted a beautiful railing on a balcony, reminiscent of what we had seen in *Samos* along the river. Then we ducked through a tunnel and met up with the alternate Camino track at *Aguiada*. It was raining pretty heavily by this time, but we were encouraged by the fact that it would not be too much longer before we reached *Sarria*.

Our calculations were correct. *Albergue A Pedra* was at the easternmost side of *Sarria*, and we found it quite easily. We were shown our room in the pension section by a very friendly host who told us that there were restaurants just a few hundred meters down the road to the west where we could eat as early as we wanted. There was no food served at the *albergue* unless one wished to use kitchen facilities which were minimal. Looked as if there were a really nice picnic area and BBQ out back, but of course the heavy rain made that unusable at the moment. We gathered some of our dirty laundry, and I went to the *albergue* section and used the washing machine there. I couldn't figure out the dryer settings, however, and our clothes did not get completely dry. So I brought them back to the room and Heather strung up our clothesline. We made do with that, hoping that everything would be dry enough by morning.

After showers and a brief nap, we set out to find the nearest restaurant. There, in a rather modern cafe with Spanish MTV blaring, we had an *Ensalada Mixta* and a pizza. Dessert was a *grande Magnum* ice cream bar. Then it was back to our room to do some Facebook posting and sleep.

Chapter Fourteen
Sarria to Santiago de Compostela

Camino No. 1 -- Day Thirty-Three: Sarria to Portomarin

At the *Hotel Alphonso IX*, breakfast did not disappoint even the fussiest of clientele, perhaps even our female friend we had run into at *Rabanal*. The buffet was enormous with lots of fresh fruit, cereals, eggs, meat and cheeses of all kinds, and of course, the omnipresent toast! While at the table, we saw the American couple come into the cafeteria. They said hello and introduced themselves as Richard and Norma. We wished them well on their Camino and said we would most likely see them later on the trail. Then we got our bags together and took them down to the lobby in time for pickup. About 9:00 am we set out for *Portomarin*. Just outside our hotel we crossed over a Romanesque bridge over the *rio Sarria* and headed up into the old section of town. Climbing up *rua Maior*, we saw a number of restaurants and shops that were of interest. We remarked that it would have been nice to stay a while longer in *Sarria* to soak some of this up, but we were due in *Portomarin* that night. At the top of the hill to the west end of town the Camino took a sharp turn downhill to the right and then crossed another river at *Ponte Aspera*. Before long, we were off into the countryside through farms lined with pristine stone walls that were hundreds of years old.

Along the way, we ran into Richard and Norma and walked with them for a good amount of time. They were very interested in hearing more about our church start in Sacramento, especially about ancient-future faith and how it corresponded with their Catholic traditions. Good conversations. Wonderful people.

We also saw the Canadian ladies we had met at the *Casa David* hotel in *Triacastela* and walked with them for a bit. They were retired travel agents who had worked together for several years and were traveling to Croatia after leaving *Santiago*. You never know who you are going to run into. By this time, we were seasoned pilgrims, and we were finding that "newbies" were really interested in what we had experienced thus far. It was fun to share stories with them, and they really appreciated our advice on a variety of topics related to the Camino. As lunch time drew closer, we could also see how crowded the Camino was becoming. Every bar and café was packed to the gills. It was good to have our own food with us. We could usually find a picnic bench with not much trouble and share it with others if need be. By the time we got past *Ferrerios*, it looked as if the rain was going to hold off, and the sun was beginning to peek through.

At the *Cruce Momientos*, I ran into the Canadian ladies, one of which was really struggling with a leg injury and was limping considerably. She was experiencing the same inner struggle that we all had and that was: "Am I going to make it?" I reassured her that she would be OK and to keep on pressing through. It wouldn't be too much further to *Portomarin*, and she could rest for the night. I caught up to Greg by this time and we descended into *Portomarin* and crossed the reservoir to the steep steps and up into the town. Our hotel, *Hotel Arenas*, was on the *Praza Condes Fenosa* and just across the street from the church of *San Nicholas*.

The street was lined with taxis on the main plaza, and I had a fleeting thought that it might be a good idea to send one back to get the Canadian woman who was struggling. My sense was though that she wanted to make it on foot, so I decided against it. We checked into the hotel and got stowed away quickly. To the left of our hotel, down the colonnaded *rua Xeral Franco*, was a great *mercado*, and Greg and I went in there and stocked up on things for the road. We saw Robert coming back from the market, and he appeared somewhat distracted. Later we saw him with a couple of guys we had never seen before who were well-dressed and definitely not pilgrims. Food was being served in the main bar area of the hotel, and we were able to get an early dinner and get to sleep at a decent hour.

Camino No. 2 -- Day Twelve: Sarria to Portomarin

As soon as we reached the top of the steps in *Sarria*, it became exceedingly apparent that the number of pilgrims had dramatically increased overnite. It seemed as if pilgrims were pouring out of every bar and stone doorway as we moved higher up the hill towards *Mosteiro da Madalena*.

Before we reached *Rua do Castelo*, we ran into Thiago coming out of one of these albergues where he had stayed the night before. He was having breakfast and spotted us passing by. It was great to see him again, and he told us his blisters were much better, although he was still moving slowly. We said goodbye and promised to look for each other later on. At the top of the hill, we kept watching all the kids being dropped off for school at *Madalena*, and missed the left turn at the *Cementario*. Heather went back up and found the turn off and I signaled to several fellow pilgrims to follow us. Then we all followed the "herd" down the steep hill and out across the old bridge over the *rio Celeiro*. The morning train into Sarria was just coming in along to the right of the path, bringing another block of pilgrims who would probably be on the Camino tomorrow.

At *Barbadelo*, we stopped at a bar/cafe for a snack and met an Austrian pilgrim who had been walking the *Camino Primitivo*. By his comments, he seemed to be highly offended by the huge crowds that we were all experiencing and was going to get a bus to *Santiago* instead of walking any further with all these noisy people. We ate our meal quickly and got back walking asap. On the way to *Morgade*, we passed through a series of small hamlets, many of which were lined with sunflower fields. Folks who had been there before us had carved faces into some of these now seedless flowers. In one of the little hamlets, Heather came across a small canine friend who had an injured paw. The little fellow was wet from the rain and turned out to be very affectionate. After following us for a 100 meters or so, his owner finally surfaced on the road and called to him.

In one of the more forested areas, we ran into Thiago again and we walked with him for a good while, talking about his life in Brazil. During this stretch, we were passed by a couple riding horses along the Camino, accompanied by two dogs who were having a great time greeting all the pilgrims.

The rain was sporadic between here and *Vilacha*, but as we got farther west, the sun seemed to be out more consistently and we put our ponchos away for good.

Just before reaching *Vilacha*, we stopped to rest on a stone wall. It was there we encountered a young couple who were looking at a site to build a new *albergue*. The couple had met on the Camino two or three years ago. He was a Spanish *hospitalero*, and she was a Danish pilgrim. They fell in love and now they were going to start their own business. They asked us what we thought of the idea of "yurts" on the Camino, particularly right at this point. We told them we had eaten dinner in a yurt in the mountains of Colorado several years ago and enjoyed the experience immensely. They seemed quite serious about their vision. We encouraged them to move forward with this idea. We said goodbye and *buen camino*.

Soon we reached the top of the hill and were ready to descend to *Portomarin*. Heather was hitting her 10-mile threshold with her thigh pain and was now starting to struggle down the hill. We stopped midway down just before the bridge over the reservoir so she could stretch for a while and then made our way farther down the road and over the long span into *Portomarin*.

As we headed up the hill into the main square, *Praza Conde de Fenosa*, I remembered the great *supermercado* I had visited on *rua Xeral Franco* amid the stone colonnades. We went in there and got some things to snack on as well as some other sundry items. Within a few minutes we were at our hotel, *Pension Arenas*.

Camino No. 1 -- Day Thirty-Four: Portomarin to Palas de Rei.

We had breakfast fairly early in the bar downstairs, and I was grateful for the two large cups of coffee that the girl from the hotel served me. It appeared to have rained during the night, an event that a lot of pilgrims probably regretted, having hung their laundry out to dry on the rooftop of the hotel. Oh well. Nasty break. While we were eating, we saw some girls who were walking together getting their rain gear on, but it looked as if it was not raining at the time. By the time we got out onto the main street to head out of town, the streets were wet, but no rain up to that point. We circled down around a large curve in the main road and crossed the bridge over the inlet to the *embalse*. Soon, we were headed up a long trail through the woods where I lost Greg once again. After a half hour up this trail, I came out to an open area along the main road that was headed towards *Toxibo*. Crossing over the street to the right side of the road, the rain suddenly came down hard, and I had to poncho up quickly. I ran into Greg before I got to *Gonzar*, and we stopped here briefly to rest at a bus stop area near a bar. It was here that we saw Richard and Norma again, and they walked with us for a couple of hours. Norma had been worried about walking these long distances when we first met her in the hotel in *Sarria*. She appeared to be doing just fine. They said that back in Ohio they were runners and often took skiing trips to various places, so they were in pretty good shape.

Greg and I stopped in *Ligonde* and found a nice picnic table and had our lunch there. In the adjoining field, there were a group of sheep feeding on the grasses and playing with their young.

The sky was getting dark again, and it looked like more rain was on the way. It was becoming somewhat annoying to keep stopping to poncho and un-poncho, but there was nothing that could be done about it due to the fact that when the sun was out, it was too steamy under the poncho. After *Eirexe*, we climbed up to *Alto Rosario* and then down for about two kilometers into the eastern outskirts of *Palas de Rei* where our hotel, *La Cabana*, was located. This was a great place that had the appearance of a mountain lodge, with outlying pine buildings housing the rooms. In the main building up front there was a big bar and dining room. I headed there as soon as I got cleaned up and had a beer and used the time to email and Facebook. Greg joined me soon thereafter, and we stayed for half hour and then went back to the room to catch our favorite TV show at 7:00 pm. At 8:00, we went back to the main building and had a good meal in the dining room that was packed by this time.

Camino No. 2 -- Day Thirteen: Portomarin to Lestedo.

I woke up at 4am this morning, got out my Galaxy TabS, and followed the Tweet feed for the Monday Night Football game of 49ers and Vikings via the NinersNation web site. By 7am, the game was over, Niners victorious, and it was time to get up and start the day. We dressed, got our bag downstairs, and walked over to the restaurant section and ate breakfast of, you guessed it, OJ, toast and coffee. Heather and I both pulled our ponchos out, certain that we would need them soon, based on weather reports we had seen, and a quick look at the skies outside the hotel through a transom window in our room.

We made our way back down the *rua Xeral Franco* and headed towards the reservoir via the twisting road across the inlet that led to the uphill track to *Toxibo*. Once again, we noted how crowded the Camino had become. There were many who passed us, still fresh from just starting their walk. "Wait another day," I told Heather. It would be at about that point that their calves and feet would begin to feel the stress of climbing and descending too fast. By the time we reached *Toxibo*, the rain was coming down steadily, and the wind was picking up speed. We had heard on TV that this weather system was part of a tropical storm that they were calling "Henri".

At *Gonzar*, we stopped at a bar for a snack, as did about 50 other pilgrims. Good for the local business. This place had their act together, being staffed sufficiently and, at least from my point of view, was providing great service to the various nationalities on the Camino with all the things we needed. More and more pilgrims were flooding into the bar and the outside area covered by a tent, so we got ourselves packed and poncho'd up and headed back on to the trail. Heather was in really good spirits, much more than I, and the rain didn't seem to bother her as much.

Soon, we crossed over the N-540 and continued upward until we reached the high point for today at *Sierra Ligonde* which is about 2,400 ft. From there it was slowly downhill through the blowing rain until we reached our destination in the little hamlet of *Lestedo* where we stayed at *Rectoral Lestedo,* a beautiful casa rural right on the Camino. A roaring fire in the lounge greeted us once we had settled in and showered. Dinner that night was truly the best we had the entire trip with a delicious roasted chicken as the main course. *Wi-Fi* was not working well in this somewhat remote location, an interesting contrast to the modernity of the establishment. The owner apologized for this inconvenience, but I was actually quite happy to be effectively cut off from everything for the evening. We met all the other guests at dinner. There was a mother and daughter from Australia, four Americans from North Carolina, and an American couple we had seen several times on the way that day who were from Newport Beach, CA. By 8pm we were flat out tired from our day's trek and needed sleep. And that we did, quite easily.

Camino No. 1 -- Day Thirty-Five: Palas de Rei to Arzua.

The main dining room had a spread that consisted of toast and jam and the rest was rather nondescript. There were no whole pieces of fruit to take with us, so we would have to make due with what we had. We finished eating, went back to the room and got our bags out and up to the main desk. It was then that the rain started coming down, and we had to run back to the room to avoid getting soaked. With our ponchos on, we headed right out of the hotel grounds and down into the town, winding our way down the slippery streets and steps to the western outskirts and across the busy N-547 and through the tiny villages of *San Xulian* and *Casanova.* There was a slippery climb out of the *rio Pambre* valley up to *Casanova* that was certainly exacerbated by the heavy rain. Since these were uphill climbs, I lost sight of Greg for about two hours until somewhere near *O Coto* where he was waiting in a shelter alongside the trail. The rain was not letting up, and we were both already soaked. Our plan was to stop at *Melide* for lunch, so we got back on the Camino and moved along as best we could. In a couple of hours, we reached *Melide* and found a little café right on the Camino. Inside, we took off our wet stuff and sat a table and ordered some food for lunch. We spent an hour here, and it was good to be out of the rain for awhile. But we had to get moving. Not far from the café, we spotted a restaurant that was serving *pulpo*. They were pulling the octopi out of the boiling pots and chopping up the tentacles right in front of us in the open window, then sprinkling it with spices and serving to the waiting customers. Greg got excited over this and I felt my stomach turning. We kept on moving through the city and found the Camino across the busy main street and up a couple of blocks. Before long, we were headed down and out of town into the rural surrounds. The rain was coming down so hard that it was nearly impossible to do anything but just keep moving. Every step produced squishing sounds, and I could only imagine what shape my blisters would be after today. I was also completely soaked up to my waist, as the rain was coming at me sideways. My poncho buttons came loose and wind took off with the poncho. A fellow pilgrim stopped to help me readjust. She and her husband were also from Ohio. They were very friendly, and we walked the rest of the way into *Arzua* together. We caught up to Greg at a bar/café near *Castaneda*, and the four of us made the final trek into *Arzua* to the *Hotel Suiza*, way on the other side of town. It was nearly six o'clock by the time we checked in, and all of us were exhausted. Up in the room, Greg and I tried to find appropriate places to put our wet clothes out to dry somehow. I found the radiator for my boots, and Greg had stuff draped all over. It took me nearly an hour to tend to my blisters and re-bandage everything. Then, as usual, I went down to the bar and had a beer and tried to get the routine for dinner. When Greg came down, we walked over to the dining room and sat down at a table. It was then that we were told that we had to make a reservation for a later time, but if we wanted to sit at the table, we could, but it would be a half hour or so before we could get service. This turned out to be much less time. Our new friends from Ohio came into the restaurant and we asked them to join us. They did, and we had a great conversation about theology. They, too, were Catholic and very interested in the liturgy of Epiclesis. Dinner was finally served to us and was quite good. I bought a good bottle of wine that we all shared. Before long, Nicolas came into the restaurant with another German that he had met along the way. They sat at another table since they had just arrived. It was another great reunion. We all said goodnight and went back to our rooms. There was only a small amount of toilet paper left in the bathroom and Greg used it all to blow his nose. This was when I began to notice that I may be coming down with what he had. I was very congested and had a terribly runny nose. I took one of the towels from the bathroom and used that through the whole night. It seemed as if I slept no more than an hour or so, after that long arduous and wet day! I prayed through the night for the rain to stop, for clothes to dry and for me not to get sick.

Camino No. 2 -- Day Fourteen: Lestedo to Melide

Rectoral Lestedo prepared a wonderful breakfast for us and we were out on the road by 8:30. Rain was intermittent, so we decided to just leave our ponchos on until we saw some sunshine. Good news was that the wind had died down somewhat so we were able to stay drier as we moved towards *Palas de Rei*. We stopped at *La Cabana* where Greg and I had stayed last trip to get some coffee, get out of the rain for a while and use the restrooms.

While there, we ran into the couple from Iceland who were doing the same thing. Good to see them again. Back on the road, we bumped into the foursome from North Carolina who were just getting to *La Cabana*, and we walked with them to *Palas de Rei*. From there, they were going to take a detour to *Castillo Pambre* so we said goodbye. The rain came down more heavily as we made our way towards the *rio Pambre*. A passing pilgrim from Australia stopped and took a picture of us.

Not too far from here, we began to see evidence of the storm. Just past the little bridge over *rio Pambre*, we stopped at *Albergue Casa Domingo* for a lunch snack. Here we met a German couple who were ordering cheeseburgers and beer!

We had our classic *bocadillo con queso* and enjoyed a delightful conversation with the Germans. After lunch, the rain had let up and we spotted the sun, so we de-poncho'd and set out to cross the delight old roman bridge.

In a few miles we were passing the *Poligono* Industrial complex and heading back into the forest before coming down the rough trail to the old bridge leading into *Furelos*.

From *Furelos*, it was a relatively short walk up the environs of *Melide*. As soon as we arrived in town, the deluge began again. By the time we got to our hotel across town, we were once again soaked.

The rain finally let up in late afternoon in *Melide*. While Heather was taking a nap in our cold room under blankets (the heat had to be turned on by the hotel staff), I ventured out into the main part of town to find an ATM and a *supermercado* to get some dark chocolate and potato chips to sustain us until dinner was served at 7:30. I found a BBVA within a few blocks and then, just around the corner, a great market that had everything I needed. Returning to the hotel, I went to the bar and ordered a large *cerveza* and a Coke zero and took them up to the room. The hot shower was a good way to get warm. Then I found another blanket and crawled under it until the heat filled the room sufficiently.

Not being too impressed with both the staff at *Pousada Chiquitin* or the facility itself, I logged on to the internet and tried to see if there were any local restaurants that were recommended. Most of them were "pulpo" (octopus) restaurants. Neither of us were particularly interested in this cuisine, nor did we want to walk a mile or so to some of the other restaurants, so we just decided to eat later in the hotel.

Soon it was time for our favorite TV show, *AhoraCaigo*, so we watched that and then went downstairs and eventually ordered a *hamburguesa* and a *ensalada mixta*. Heather said the salad was OK and, from my point of view, the hamburger was marginal, at best. A blah evening, 180 degrees from last night, but we were safe and warm (by now) and thankful for that.

The street outside the hotel was all torn up with construction that appeared to be installation of new sewer and water lines. The work went on until darkness fell and began early in the morning.

Camino No. 2 -- Day Fifteen: Melide to Arzua

In the cold wet morning, we set out for *Arzua*. The day was rather uneventful, and the rain came and went throughout the morning. Just east of *Ribadiso*, the sun began to peak through the clouds, and we removed our ponchos for good. We crossed over the little bridge by the *albergue Xunta* and criss-crossed the N547 until we made it up the hill to *Arzua* until we eventually found *Via Lactea*. Our beds were in a 16-bed dorm. Heather took the lower bunk and I the upper. There was a laundry facility in the back of the *albergue*, and we gathered everything, got some Euro coin, and proceeded to wash what we could. No soap was for sale in any vending machine, but I was able to scrape some bits from a bin that I found and that would have to do. This part of the *albergue* was freezing. I found some blankets, and we sat on an old sofa in this dank room, all bundled up, and gritted our teeth with wry laughter.

After the laundry was finished, we folded everything up and put it away in our bag. Then we set out to the main part of town to get something to eat. On *Calle Lugo*, outside *Casa Teodoro*, we ran into the mother and daughter from Australia. They were staying at the hotel and just going out to do a little shopping before dinner. We chatted for a while and laughed at our aching muscles. They took off for sightseeing and shopping and we decided to eat at *Casa Teodoro*. This turned out to be a good choice. It was a busy and very comfortable restaurant. Heather had a great salad, and I opted for *pimientos padron* and a cheese plate *con pan*. Excellent food with a good glass of wine and a fine Coke Zero! After the meal, we strolled through the town since the rain had stopped and tried to find someplace that was selling ice cream. No luck, so we made our way back through the narrow streets to our dreary *albergue* and hid ourselves away in our corner bunk. Before long, it was time to try and sleep which was a challenge due to a soccer game playing on TV at some remote part of the establishment with a rowdy group of men cheering some team on until 11 pm. As soon as that was over, things quieted down to some extent except for some room mates that came in late and were making a lot of noise settling in next to us.

When we woke up in the morning, we were both tired from the lack of sleep and Heather had a bad headache. At the crack of dawn, we set out via the back roads of town through the adjacent forest towards *Arca*, our next stop.

Camino No. 1 -- Day Thirty-Six: Arzua to O' Pedrouza (Arca)

Breakfast was very good in the dining room with fresh juice and good jams. We saw our Ohio friends and Nicolas in the lobby getting ready to go. When we got back down there, it appeared that they had already taken off, and we didn't see them the rest of the day. Since our hotel was on the far end of town, we only had to go about 100 yards up the main road and take a path to the left that led us directly to the Camino. The rain held off for most of the day, and we went through a series of small farm towns. The Italian biker near *O'Cebreiro* had told me that I would be able to smell the sea, but all I could smell now was manure. More and more I was content just to know that it would be only a couple of days longer before I got to *Santiago*. That's what kept me going in spite of the pain from the blisters.

By mid-afternoon, the sun was out, and the rest of the day was pleasant. After climbing up to *Alto de Santa Irene*, we came down into the village of *Santa Irene* and down a long hill to *A Rua*.

Greg and I passed the tourist information building there and decided to keep moving to the main town of *Arca do Pino (O'Pedrouza)* where we would find our hotel. When we reached the outskirts of town, we stopped at a *Repsol* gas station and decided to ask someone there for directions to the hotel which was called *Casa da Agua*. Greg waited outside while I went in to see what I could find. After determining that the attendant spoke no English, I pulled out the voucher as I was asking him in my rudimentary Spanish,

"Donde esta la *Casa da Agua*, por favor".

He shrugged and picked up his phone and dialed a number. I wasn't certain he had heard my request and I was attempting to shove the voucher in his direction when he held up his hand to stop me and he began to converse with someone on the other end of his phone. When he hung up, I said

"*Casa da Agua*?"

"Si senor, *Casa da Agua*"

"Donde esta" I replied.

"Aqui, senor" as he pointed to the station office in which we were standing.

"*Casa da Agua* esta aqui?"

"Si, aqui. Diez minuto, aqui."

Then he abruptly returned to his duties as gas attendant.

So, it appeared that he had called someone from the *Casa da Agua* who would be here in ten minutes. I went outside and relayed this information to Greg who was skeptical. He thought that the attendant had called a cab for us who would then come and pick us up and take us a few blocks to town and drop us off at the hotel and charge us a fortune for it, when we could just as easily walk there. Greg suggested that we just keep moving and walk into town and find the hotel on our own. My thought was that perhaps the attendant had indeed called the hotel owner and that it would be rude to have him come all this way to find no one around. Greg assented, and we decided to wait for ten minutes and then proceed.

As I examined the hotel voucher again, I noticed that there were no general directions as there had been with previous vouchers.

While we waited, we watched other pilgrims pass on their way into Arco. Some we recognized and they waived to us. With every car that pulled into the station, we thought our mysterious driver might be here at last, but they were just filling up on petrol. Soon, a small white sedan zipped in and came to an abrupt stop. The driver got out and walked quickly to the rear of the car and opened the trunk. I approached him and said *"Casa da Agua?"* The stocky middle-aged man grunted in the affirmative and motioned us over. He took our backpacks and put them in the trunk. Greg got in the back seat and I sat up front with the driver. He backed around nimbly and headed out of the station onto the main road. It soon became apparent that he spoke no English as well, and his Spanish was textured with a heavy *Galician* dialect. So, communication was going to be difficult. Shortly, after we set out into town, I asked once more, *"Casa da Agua, si?"* "Si, si," was his reply. I looked back at Greg and he just smiled and shrugged his shoulders. We drove through town and took a right. After about a hundred yards, the driver pointed to a path leading through the woods and uttered, "Alli, el Camino, amigo" I thought I saw a Camino directional sign and nodded affirmatively to the driver. In less than a minute we were out of town and headed deep into the woods.

A five-minute drive through dense pines and eucalyptus trees brought us to an intersection with a main highway which we crossed and proceeded further into the woods. After a mile or so, the forest gave way to a wide expanse of hilly farmland, dotted with cottonwoods and sycamores. Our driver began to explain things to us about the surrounding area. He gestured to buildings and churches and explained something about them, none of which we understood. By now, it was clear that we were miles from the Camino and my imagination was getting the best of me. A modicum of fear began to enter my consciousness. I looked back at Greg with a non-verbal "I don't know" sort of expression and he seemed to be feeling the same way. I began concocting all sorts of stories in my mind, like was this abrupt fellow, pleasant as he was, taking advantage of these two tired pilgrims? Worse yet, were we going to some sort of rendezvous with some other bad guys who might try to roll us? Sizing up the driver, I figured that Greg and I together could take him if he tried something. That is, of course, unless he was armed, and if that were the case, we were clearly up the proverbial creek. And yes, what if he had accomplices wherever he was taking us? Had we walked all this way from France to come to this end? I closed my eyes and briefly prayed for protection until that was interrupted by more incoherent descriptions of things that we were passing. I nodded, trying to show some gratitude for this "guided tour." Finally, after several twists and turns on very narrow roads that produced no reduction in speed, we reached what appeared to be a farmhouse that was set on a picturesque hill. We pulled in the driveway and drove around to the rear of an old stone house that appeared to have some modern additions to it. Our strange driver turned off the ignition and said, "*Casa da Agua!*"

There were no external signs to indicate hotel or Casa Rural. Greg came up with the understatement of the trip, "Well, we would never have found this place!" From the gas station, it was about a fifteen-minute drive, I figured. As we retrieved our packs from the trunk, and followed the man inside, it soon became apparent that he was indeed our host. He directed us into a small lobby that had a high desk and telephone and asked for our passports, making some remarks that seemed to indicate that he could take care of the formalities later and leave our passports at the desk. He was now intent on showing us around the place. The interior of the old house had been remodeled within the last few years, and it was indeed a wonderful job. Stairways and parts of the house were blended with the old stone walls that produced a rustic but Frank Lloyd Wright sort of feel. After a brief tour of the downstairs area, the man led us up the stairs to our room. As we moved down a wood-paneled hallway with tile floors covered by occasional rugs, we came to our room. Our guest opened the door, and there was Greg's bag sitting on a luggage rack! I was suddenly relieved more that I can say. The man then motioned us to a room next door and opened that door. There was my bag too. It appeared we each had our own room. The man asked me something about la cena that I couldn't quite understand. I responded with "A que hora est la Cena?" More incoherent responses from our host until he finally settled on "Ocho hora, senor?" "Si, bueno," I replied. After giving me a key to the entrance door of the house, our host scurried off to the downstairs area. Greg and I stood there in the hallway, stunned, greatly relieved, and just really amused by the entire situation. By now it was about five pm. We decided to retire to our rooms and get showers and take a nap before dinner at eight o'clock.

The bathroom was arguably the best one we had encountered on the entire trip with the possible exception of the *Hotel Carris Alphonso IX* in *Sarria*. I turned the towel warmer on, washed my sole-surviving handkerchief and hung it up to dry. After the blister bandage-removal ritual I had come to know and love (*ha!*), I stepped into a hot and soothing shower, dried off, and put on some clean clothes. I was enjoying my own private room and stretched out on one of the two queen-sized beds. Before long, I had fallen asleep. At 6:30, I woke up and ventured out into the upper reaches of the guest house. In a stunning living room at the far end of the house, there were great clear views through wall-to-wall windows of the hills we had traversed all the way from *Melide* to this point. There was no available Wi-Fi so I just snapped some pictures of this part of the house and returned to my room to get ready for dinner. This involved most importantly, the bandage application ritual which would carry me through the evening and all the next day. It occurred to me that this would probably be the last of these detailed procedures, and oddly enough that thought was met with mixed emotions.

At about 7:30, there was a knock at the door. It was our host who let me know something about dinner amid some confusing gestures and then scurried off downstairs once again. Before leaving, he tapped his wristwatch, muttered "ocho hora" once more, and I nodded as if I understood. Gathering my rainproof jacket and a fleece top, I knocked on Greg's door. He was awake and fairly ready to go. While he was finishing getting dressed, we joked about the bizarre happenings of the day and then headed downstairs. At the desk we found our passports in a neat pile, but no sign of our host anywhere. I also found a stamp and an ink pad at the desk and stamped both our pilgrim *credencials* (passports) with the Casa da Agua *sello* (stamp). By now it was clear that we were the only people in the guest house! We decided to scout around and see more of the place and were able to determine that there were two wings in the upstairs living area that had about eight rooms each. Downstairs there was a large dining room that would probably seat 50 people if it was packed full. Nothing was set out for dinner, and there was no sign or smell of anything happening. Back near the desk area we found a formal guest book that had been signed by people from all parts of the world. Some of the comments that we could read also referred to the fact that they were the only people in the house at the time. Greg and I pondered this from an economic viewpoint and resigned ourselves to the fact that it, as well as many other things we had experienced in Spain, made no sense at all. At the other side of the room that contained the desk was a large walk-in fireplace that showed no signs of any recent fire as well as a huge cooking grill in the center of the room with a big vent above it. It, too, appeared to have not been used for quite some time. Greg wanted to check the entrance area at the back of the house where we came in earlier to see if there was a soda machine. We stepped outside and found nothing of the sort. Back inside, we noticed that it was eerily quiet and I felt as if we had stepped into an episode of the Twilight Zone or, more appropriately, a chapter in a Bram Stoker novel.

Suddenly, Greg looked over my shoulder out the window towards the road we had come in on and asked me, "Hey, Don, what kind of car was that guy driving when he brought us here?"

"It was a little white sedan"

"Well there is a little black sedan just pulling up out by the road. Our guy is talking to the driver. And now it looks as if he is motioning us to come up there"

We stepped out the back entrance door and made our way around the side and up the path to the waiting car. Our host opened the passenger side doors for us and we got in. "Por la cena?" in my broken Spanish. "Si, senor"

We sat there for a couple of minutes while our host talked with the driver about some other subject entirely. They both laughed and finally our host stepped back and the driver put the car in gear and sped off. "I take you to dinner, amigos", he said. "Bueno", I replied, then looked back at Greg who was giving the thumbs up sign. Things were beginning to make sense. Since we were the only people staying at the guest house, there was obviously another place we were to go to eat. This was not unusual for us since there had been several hotels along the way at which we had stayed that did not serve dinner. We were then directed to restaurants nearby that were often really good options where the food was delicious. But, being out in the middle of nowhere, our host had arranged for someone to come and take us to a restaurant somewhere. That was probably what he was explaining to me earlier that I was unable to understand. The driver was pleasant enough, and his English turned out to be better than our host. He, too, seemed to enjoy pointing out various historical buildings and spinning some stories about them. I was able to catch most of it. The drive to the restaurant lasted about 10 minutes and we arrived at the *Hotel Bello* in the little town of *Santiso*.

The driver led us inside to the bar area of the restaurant and gave some instructions to the bartender who appeared to be quite deferential to the driver. Then the driver looked at me and said that he would be back when we had finished so as to drive us back to the guest house. It was then, to our great surprise, that we noticed that there was one other "special" guest in the *Hotel Bello*. It was Robert, who Greg and I had referred to as Gandhi, because he bore a striking resemblance to him. We first met him in the remote town of *Calzdilla de la Cueza* about 17 days earlier at a communal dinner that evening in the hotel. He appeared to have been traveling with a young lady from Norway who had two dogs with her. West of *Astorga*, we saw him alone in the village of *Murias de Rechivaldo*. Greg asked him what had happened to the girl with the dogs. Gandhi told us that they had split up walking together because she wanted to go much faster and he wanted to take more time. We saw him the next day at *Cruz de Ferro* and he offered to take our picture with my smart phone. Greg engaged him in conversation and Gandhi began to pontificate about the problems in the world all being the result of corrupt institutions. I interjected that in my opinion the problem was evil in the world. Gandhi told me that only about 15% of the world is evil and that could be handled. The conversation went no further. Others that we had met on the trail remarked about meeting this "interesting" person. "I think his name is Robert," said a chap from North Carolina that I walked from *O'Cebriero* to *Triacastela* with.

Since recognizing him was somewhat unavoidable, we opted on the side of being cordial and said hello. Gandhi seemed to be a bit preoccupied, writing in what appeared to be a journal. He smiled and said hello. Apparently, he had booked this room in the *Hotel Bello* and taken a cab from *Santa Irene*. At this point, the bartender, who turned out to also be the waiter in the restaurant, and showed us to a table. Everybody in this part of the world seemed to be multi-tasking.

Moments later Gandhi walked up to our table and asked if he could join us for dinner. We both sensed that it would be rude to refuse since there was absolutely no one else in the restaurant and we asked the waiter if we could move to a larger table. Gandhi confirmed to us his name was indeed Robert, and remembered meeting us a while back on the trail. Obviously, we left much less of an impression on him that he had left on us. Then, to our surprise, he told us that a lot of people called him "Gandhi Ji" because of his resemblance to the great Indian Leader. Greg and I both chuckled to ourselves on this one.

As it turned out, Robert proved to be a delightful dinner companion. He was from *Sydney*, Australia and had been a CFO for an international corporation with clients all over the world. Now retired, he was on the payroll as a consultant of several international clients that he had worked with throughout his career. He would travel on assignment for two to three months out of the year and spend the rest of the time going on adventures such as the *Camino de Santiago*. He also regaled us of his travels on other pilgrimages that he had taken to *Jerusalem*, to various shrines in Europe, and to *Mecca*! After resting in Santiago for a few days, he was going to walk the *Camino Portuguese* backwards to *Lisbon*. He was married and showed us pictures of his wife back in *Sydney*. She would join him in *Lisbon* and they would vacation together for a couple of weeks. At one point, Robert went up to his room and returned with some cold medicine that he gave to me because I was complaining of symptoms that I was having from the night before. Robert told us that he believed that his hands were healing hands, but this was not credited to the Holy Spirit. He had learned the "art of massage" and acupressure. Along the way, he claimed to have "ministered" to several people who were able to "heal" overnight and make it back out on the Camino. I mentioned we had last seen him on the street in

Portomarin. He told us that night was his birthday and that one of his clients had flown his private jet to *Santiago* and rented a limousine at the airport and drove to *Portomarin* to surprise him for his birthday. Robert told us that the client was a wealthy Middle Eastern businessman who brought a gift of a new watch for him.

Our dinner was indeed delicious. Robert and Greg had "pulpo", which is a local Galician specialty. It is actually octopus, suction cups and all! For me, it was steak, which was wonderful, along with some red potatoes in a really good sauce. We all shared a bottle of *vino tinto*, and after some fruit and flan for dessert we settled up the dinner bill and said good evening. I thanked Robert once again for the cold medicine, and he headed up to his room. Our driver was waiting for us in the bar and showed us outside to the car for the trip home to the *Casa da Agua*. It turned out that the driver was indeed the owner of the *Hotel Bello* and that he and our *Casa da Agua* host were good friends. The sun was beginning to set by now, and we thoroughly enjoyed the ride to the guest house. After thanking "Senor Bello" for the ride and the great meal in his restaurant, we let ourselves in with the key our host had given me and hit the sack for a well-deserved sleep.

Camino No. 2 -- Day Sixteen: Arzua to O'Pedrouza (Arca)

We were awoken before the sun was up by our noisy neighbors in the adjoining bunks, but this was OK with Heather and I, because we couldn't wait to get out of this place and back on the trail. What a crummy night! It didn't take long to pack up and make our way to *Rua do Carmen* and out of town into the forest. Once we were in the woods, it became darker but we could see well enough. About a half mile up the trail, I noticed the track to the right that led to *Hotel Suiza* where Greg and I had stayed last trip. Approaching *Pregontono*, the sun was rising in spectacular fashion and Heather got a great picture:

At *A Peroxa*, we stopped at a cozy bar for some breakfast where we encountered a very friendly and efficient staff. Here, we also ran into a young German friend, Marie, from *Berlin*, who we had met the day before. It was great to see her again.

During the climb up to *Salceda*, we met an elderly South African man who had been on several pilgrimages. He was moving in a very labored manner up the wet, muddy path and we walked with him for a while listening to his tales as he told us in great detail what he intended to eat for dinner in *Santa Irene*. After a while, this became a little tedious and we said goodbye and moved on. He was very good-humored about it, however. Later, when I stopped to use the outdoor facilities, he caught up to us and was bending Heather's ear once again. We chuckled about this encounter for the rest of the day. While we were heading up into the town, we came across two young women, one of whom was struggling with a painful leg problem. Heather stopped to help her and offered some advice for using kinesiology tape that she might be able to download via the internet. She was thankful for that, but thought she could make it OK. We stopped at a rest area along the road in *Salceda* and ate some fruit and nuts. This would be our lunch for the day. The sunshine felt good, and it warmed us as we sat on a comfortable bench and watched other pilgrims pass us by.

At the outskirts of *Salceda,* we began another long climb and soon we were at the high altitude point for the day at *Alto Santa Irene*. Then we began the steep descent to the *rio Burgo* and into *Arca*. As we entered the busy town, I pointed out the *Respol* gas station where Greg and I had called for help in getting to *Casa da Agua* two years earlier. We proceeded up the busy street into town, stopped at a *supermercado* to get some snacks, and then quickly found our hostal, *Pension A Solaina*, with little problem. Our host was quite helpful in getting us to our room and settled in. This was a great place, located right in the center of town. The room was quite modern, and the bathroom was spectacular. Hot showers followed quickly and we both took brief naps before venturing out for some food.

At the entrance to the town, we remembered passing some restaurants, so we decided to head there first and see what we could find. We settled on a modern Italian joint and ordered a pizza. While waiting for our meal, we noticed two of the Australian men that were in the group with Vince and Henrietta. I waved to them and one of the guys came in and said hello. He told us that they were probably going to be in big trouble with their wives because they were drinking beer in a bar and missed the ride to the *casa rural* where they were all staying. They had to arrange alternate transportation and were waiting for the taxi to arrive to pick them up. While waiting, of course, they were downing a couple of additional beers! Haha! We said goodbye to them, and they said they would convey our regards to Vince and Henrietta. Our pizza came and we devoured it quite easily. Of course, we just had to have our chocolate Magnum Ice Cream bars for dessert. Then we were ready to head back to the pension and hole up for the night, grateful that we had made it this far, and that tomorrow we would be in *Santiago*. Woohoo!

Camino No. 1 -- Day Thirty-Seven, O'Pedrouza to Santiago

In the morning, we packed up our gear and brought our bags downstairs as we had been accustomed to doing so often. We could smell coffee brewing and soon noticed that our host was beckoning us towards the dining room where he had laid out a wonderful spread of fruit, jam, meats and cheese as well as scrambled eggs. Still just the two of us in the whole place. After we had taken some fruit and bread for the walk into Santiago, our host came by the table and gave us a DVD of *"Casa da Agua"* in English for which I thanked him and then packed it away in my backpack. A half hour later we were on our way back to *O'Pedrouza* where our host stopped the car at the entrance to the Camino. We said goodbye, and as we watched him drive off, I wondered if I had ever experienced a more interesting 16 hours filled with so much intrigue and delightful surprises.

Within a few minutes, we were deep into a beautiful Eucalyptus forest as we headed towards our final destination. As I walked along, I was thinking that today I would be in *Santiago* without a doubt. In other words, I was definitely going to make it all the way. I felt as if I could crawl there if need be and still make it. Up until this point in time, the question was in doubt. Something could always happen that might prevent me from completing the trip. I could now say with confidence that nothing would stop me from reaching the end of the journey. Greg got out ahead soon, as usual, and I lagged along enjoying the forest. In the little village of *San Anton*, I met two young girls from America who worked for the Peace Corps and were on a holiday and decided to walk the Camino from *Sarria* to *Santiago*. They were delightful young women and I enjoyed a ten-minute walk with them before they stopped to have a snack. At the end of the forest, before it opened into the fields surrounding *Amenal*, I stopped to take care of some lingering business.

Getting back underway, I took the tunnel under the N-547, emerged, and started the long, slow climb up to the *Santiago* Airport in *Lavacolla*. For the most of the morning, I was alone on this trail that was similar to the California foothills with pine trees dotting the landscape.

After maneuvering around the airport, the trail took a sharp turn to the right. It was here I found Greg waiting for me, and we walked through the little hamlet of *San Paio* before crossing under the N-634a via a tunnel. The Camino then led us through the environs of *Lavacolla*, and shortly we crossed back over the highway that went directly through the main part of town to head up to *Vilamaior*.

That was a steep climb in many sections until we got to the TV station and a sharp turn to the left and a campground that had a snack bar. We stopped here and ate the fruit and snacks that we had accumulated. While sitting there, it occurred to us that this would likely be the last lunch of this type we would have on our trip.

By this time, there appeared to be a non-stop flow of pilgrims that walked past us as we sat there, and I found myself wondering how crowded the city would be. After lunch, we took a short zig-zag and then down a long paved street to the little village of *San Marcos*. At the end of the town and up a small hill we arrived at *Monte del Gozo* which overlooks the city and has a monument that has become iconic. There were tour buses, school children, and bicycle clubs here swarming around the monument, and it seemed a bit like Disneyland.

We spent about ten minutes at *Gozo* and then took off down the hill towards *Santiago*. On the way, there were many local walkers who had joined up, so it was a rather jovial walk down. When we reached the end of the hill, we crossed over the RR tracks via an old wooden walkway and into the city environs.

From there it was a matter of winding our way through the city streets, past the statue of the Knight Templar, all the while keeping an eye on the Camino markings in the pavement, until we reached the *Porto Do Camino* and eventually made through the narrow streets to *Prazo Obradoiro* and the magnificent *Santiago* Cathedral. An unusal street band, playing semi-classical pieces greeted us as we entered the plaza around at the side. We stopped for a while to listen to the accordion, mandolin and bass and soak in the atmosphere.

Then we dipped down the steps to the main square fronting the Cathedral. I was flooded with emotions, realizing that I had longed for this day for quite a while now. Pilgrims were all over the place hugging each other and recognizing those that they had met along the way and from whom they had become separated.

We didn't see any of our "folks", but were certain that they would turn up sooner or later. After watching this scene for a bit, we may our way west down *Rua Hortas* and up the steps to *Rua do Pombal* to our hotel for the next two nights. Inside, the desk clerk informed us that we had been switched to another hotel, but not to worry because the new place was even nicer than where we were. She told us that the hotel was owned by the same corporation and that they would call a cab for us and pay for it. That seemed fine to us and we waited outside for the cab which came right away. The new hotel was called *Hotel Virxe de Cerca* and was really nice. Our room was big and had three beds. It was also just off a beautiful garden area which also led to the dining area and the bar off a pleasant patio.

After stowing our gear, we took showers and then proceeded back to the Cathedral area to find the Pilgrim Office to have our passports stamped and to receive our *compostelas*. This was located in the *Casa do Dean* on *Rua Vilar*. It was quite crowded with pilgrims lining up to do the same thing.

Again there were many reunions happening as we waited in line. Once inside the door, there was a long winding line up a staircase that led to the upper doors and cubby holes where the officials were to ask questions and stamp our passports. They also wrote out our information on the *compostelas*, and handed them to us while congratulating us at the same time.

On the way out, we both purchased tubes to preserve the *compostelas* properly so we could pack them away in our bags without getting them damaged or torn. We left from here and went back to the hotel for a nap and after that a drink at the bar where a very friendly barkeeper gave us some local history. By seven o'clock we were out on the streets looking for a restaurant to get an "early" meal. We found one on the *Praza Cervantes*, and although it was already packed with a rowdy crowd, there was a small table near the rear of the place that we could snare. The menu was primarily Italian, and we found it delicious. Darkness was now descending on the city, and we returned to our room and got to bed early.

Camino No 2 -- Day 17: O'Pedrouza to Santiago de Compostella

Just five minutes from *Pension A Solaina*, we found *Bar El Mundo* and stopped in for some toast and coffee before heading into the forest to *San Anton*. During this stretch, we met a delightful nun who was walking alone, so we spent several minutes talking with her as we proceeded through these eucalyptus groves. The morning was still chilly, but the sky was a bright blue. I was so grateful that we would have such a beautiful day to walk into *Santiago*. Answered prayer!

We went through the *Amenal Tunel* under the N-547 and then made the long climb up to the airport and around to *San Paio*. At the top of the hill in *Vilamaior*, we stopped for lunch at a nice albergue/bar. Refreshed from this, we moved on past the TV station, down the hill to *San Marcos* and were soon at *Monte de Gozo* and the monument commemorating the visit of Pope John Paul II.

I wanted to cross over the adjacent park area to find the Pilgrim statues that I had missed on the last trip, so we spent an extra ten minutes heading south to find them. When we got there, there was a bus load of tourists who were swarming all over the place so we had to wait until they were gone to get some good pictures. This was somewhat annoying, but we were careful to remind ourselves that they had as much right to be there as we did. This little side trip did not disappoint.

After the statue experience, we hiked back to the monument and got a Magnum chocolate bar for two Euros at the snack bar and then headed down the hill to the city. In a few minutes we were crossing over the train tracks on the rickety foot bridge into the environs of *Santiago*. We stopped to rest at a bench on *Rua San Pedro*, then picked up the Camino through the narrow streets to *Praza Obradoiro*.

Coming down the stairs through the archway leading to the plaza, we were greeted by a bagpiper who was playing an intermittent salute to all the pilgrims. Then it was into the huge open space in front of the west face of the Cathedral. As all pilgrims know, this is a very emotional time. Heather was overcome and fell to her knees sobbing, so thankful that she had had made it.

After we had given thanks for our journey, I took my backpack off and hoisted it above in a victory celebration. Heather took off her shoes because she felt she was on holy ground. We got some good pictures of her heavily bandaged feet. By now, she had blisters on every toe.

After resting for a long time on the stone plaza, we walked back up through the archway to our hotel, *Hospederia San Martin Pinerio* and checked in. Our room was small and somewhat sparse, but it was extremely clean and comfortable with a modernized bathroom. After an hour or so we cleaned up and set out for the Pilgrim's office at *Casa do Dean* on *Rua Vilar*. The line was very long and hardly moving so we decided to come back in the morning when it might be easier to get through. As we were standing there, the Australian mother/daughter duo were coming out. They had just received their *compostelas* and were brimming with happiness. We also saw the nun that we had met earlier in the day near *San Anton* and she was trying to find some fellow nuns that were working at *Casa do Dean*.

Heather and I left the Pilgrim's office and headed back up the stairs to *Plaza Quintana* and checked out a few souvenir shops before returning to the hotel. We stopped at the cafeteria/bar before going up to the room and picked up a snack and drink. Then, it was nap time until we went down for dinner about 8:00.

Chapter Fifteen

Santiago de Compostela

Camino No. 1 – Day 38, Santiago de Compostela

At breakfast in the morning, we were surprised to see the two gals from Canada that we had first met in *Triacastela*. They had made it in later yesterday, and they were glad to see us. There were also a bunch of Americans in the dining area who were on a guided tour and had been walking pieces of the Camino from Sarria on in. These were most likely the people we saw from time to time getting on and off buses that were strategically waiting before long uphill climbs. They seemed anxious to meet us, and fascinated by the fact that we had walked the entire 500 miles. Greg and I found that we had become minor celebrities in the hotel, as other tourists came up to us saying that they had heard about us from their friends. We both found this quite amusing and almost a bit annoying, but we were careful to be accommodating to all of them.

At 10:30 am we set out for the Cathedral to go to the Pilgrim Mass that was scheduled for noon, intending to get there early for a seat up close and hoping to see the *botafumeria* in action. People were sitting in pews that spiked out in four directions from the centrally-located altar. There was plenty of time to take a tour of the cathedral, but we feared that we would lose our seats, so Greg went on the tour while I saved us two seats. One of the guards spoke to me about taking pictures. It seemed that I was sitting in the prayer area, and there was no picture-taking allowed there. I apologized and moved to another location that actually had a better view of the altar. When I saw Greg, I flagged him down and he came over to where I was. It was then that I saw the Irish couple sitting across the way in the praying area. I went over there to say hello, and they were really glad to see me. We decided to find each other after the service since they were really frowning on people talking. Then I did a quick mini-tour of the cathedral primarily wanting to see the tomb of St. James.

It was getting close to noon by now, so I returned to our seats where Greg was holding forth. I figured I could see anything I wanted later after the mass. Out of nowhere, Nicolas appeared, and we were really happy to see him. He couldn't find the fellow he had been travelling with, so we asked him to join us, and he did. Nicolas brought us up to date on everyone that he had seen in the last couple of days and we did the same with him. He had run into Priscilla, who was arriving in *Santiago* today, but had to get the airport to catch a plane late in the afternoon. She was not going to be able to attend the mass. Soon it was time for the mass to begin. It was great having Nicolas there because he was able to explain a lot of the liturgy to us which was in either Spanish or Latin. At an early point, there was a welcoming of all the pilgrims and a list of all the countries they represented. After this, a British chap spoke, representing an Anglican group that had made the pilgrimage. He brought a present for the church in *Santiago*. It was incense from England. The head priest gladly received the gift and placed it on the altar. I found myself hoping that they would swing the *botafumeria* for sure now.

The mass went on, and they served communion. Apparently there were too many in attendance to have all the congregants take the wine, so they only offered the bread to all of us. The priests blessed the wine and took it for all of us. Greg and I went up to get a wafer and a blessing from one of the priests. After that there was a passing of the peace which was quite moving. There were pilgrims of many religious traditions from all over the world, literally, as well as locals who regularly worshipped at the church hugging each other saying "may the peace of Christ be with you". Then the head priest said in English that "we are all brothers and sisters through Christ our Savior". After some liturgical singing in Latin, they brought the *botafumeria* to the center of the altar and lowered it to fill it up with incense. After it was lit, the seven monks manned the ropes and pulled it up so it could swing through the church. Everyone was getting pictures of this, and the guards did not seem to mind. Both Greg and I took videos of this amazing event, something neither of us will ever forget.

When the service was finished, the doors to the sides were opened so people could get out easier. Greg and I said goodbye to Nicolas, who was catching a plane to Germany later in the day. He would be home this evening. Greg and I wished it would be that easy for us. Due to the large crowds, it was impossible to locate our Irish friends, so we just hung on inside the church and did a bit more touring. Outside the Cathedral, there was a steady stream of pilgrims coming into the city.

Greg and I visited a number of shops to search for some souvenirs to bring home. I bought Heather a necklace, and Greg was intent on finding a brass shell that he could place in cement at his house. I left him in the shops after a while and went to sit on the wall near the Cathedral and watch the pilgrims enter the city. Across the way, the trio I had seen earlier was beginning to play and I made a video of this. On another corner was a musician playing a sitar.

Greg came back from shopping and we found a small restaurant on *Rua Vilar* and had some lunch. After that we returned to the hotel to get some sleep. Still trying to catch up, I guess. When I woke up, I went down to the bar/lounge and ordered a glass of *vino tinto* and took it to a comfortable chair in the library area.

While there, I met another woman from Ohio that was part of the tour group I had seen at breakfast. She explained that she was a Catholic sister, known as Sister Carol, and she was talking to her priest back home via Skype. When she was finished, we struck up a conversation. It turns out she was part of a bus tour that started in *O'Cebreiro,* and she was interested in meeting pilgrims who had walked the whole way from *St. Jean Pied de Port.* We talked for several minutes and then she asked me if I had received the Pilgrim's Blessing when I passed through *O'Cebriero*. When I explained how tired I was at the end of the long 17-mile climb up the mountain, how I had crawled into the shower, spent an hour dressing my two enormous heel blisters, hobbled down to the restaurant for a pilgrim's menu, and then crawled back up the steps to my room and into bed, I think she understood why I had no strength left to go searching for the chapel at *Santa Maria a Real* and stay up for the Vesper Service that night. "Oh well," she said, "I guess you might like to have one of these cards that I got in the gift shop at the church there." She handed me the post card. "Keep it," she said. "I have another. May the Lord bless you from this day forward." I thanked her and very briefly glanced at the card, then continued the conversation for several more minutes.

"Don't you feel as if you have really accomplished something, walking 500 miles to Santiago and completing this pilgrimage that is over 1,200 years old!", she asked. I told her that I really did not feel as though I had done anything extraordinary, because there were so many others who had come before me and so many who were also with me on the road. But I told her that I could not have accomplished the walk without the grace of God and all the prayers of the saints. I told her about my thoughts and feelings as I was nearing the top of the mountain – how my body was beginning to give out from exhaustion, but when looking back at the magnificent mountain range I had just come through, that at this vantage point, I felt it would be a good place to die. We laughed together and said goodbye. Some other activities distracted me immediately after, and I just stuck the card in my pocket. It wasn't until after I got home, days later, that I found the card. It was tucked away in my collection of memorabilia that was stuffed into my diary. I pulled it out and read it in its entirety. Just one more blessing from the Camino.

I sat there for a while emailing Heather and posting some pictures of the day on Facebook. Five minutes later, and much to my surprise, Richard and Norma came bouncing down the steps into the library. They were staying here in the hotel, and it was another nice reunion. They had arrived yesterday as well and got up early today and took the tour to *Finesterre* by bus. We adjourned to the bar and had a drink to share the experiences of the last three days. I had not seen them since early on the road to *Palas da Rei*, so much had taken place. They asked me about the mass, and I told them that they would need to get there early to get a good seat. While we were talking, Sister Carol came by once again and I introduced everyone. Carol joined us for a short time and told us about one of the members of her tour group who was a "skeptic" and was suffering some severe anger and depression issues. We prayed for her right there in the bar at the table. Carol got up after that and went to join some others while Richard, Norma and I continued our conversation. Soon Greg joined us, and we spent the better part of the next hour just having a great time. Richard and Norma then wanted to go up to their room and get cleaned up and rested before they went out to dinner. On the way back to the room to get our things to go out to dinner, I found an interesting sculpture that reminded me of Heather and me. It was just off the walkway from our room that bordered the beautiful garden area.

Within a few minutes, Greg and I were off to find the restaurant that was owned by *Pousadas de Compostela*, the chain that owned the hotel where we were staying. We had a special coupon provided by the hotel and we wanted to make good use of it. We found the place, but it was already packed. Near the door, one of the waiters told us that they were opening the downstairs dining area in a few minutes and that we could go down there. Soon we had our menus delivered, and we could make no sense of them. This was getting old to me by this time. I just wanted to get a good meal, get back to the hotel and a good night's sleep before a long day's trip tomorrow back to California. I asked the waiter if he could explain the menu and he could speak no English. I told him I wanted *carne*, and he pointed to various menu items and then to a different part of his body to illustrate where the meat came from. I took the butt area, and Greg broke out laughing uproariously. When my meal came, it was too raw to eat. I complained to the waiter who indicated that he had a solution. In a short time, he came back with a huge stone that he was holding with enormous pot holders. He set the stone down next to my plate and indicated that I should put the meat on the stone to cook it more. That solved the problem and meal was great. On the way back from the restaurant, we saw a guy with a big ice cream cone. We asked him where he got it and then went there and got one for ourselves. Feeling quite satisfied, we returned to the hotel and went to bed.

Camino No. 2 – Day 18, Santiago de Compostela

Even though we did not have to be anywhere early today, we were still up by 7:30 and headed downstairs to experience our first breakfast at *Hospederia San Martin Pinerio*. This was by far the best breakfast buffet we experienced on the Camino! The large room was bustling with excitement as pilgrims were clearly enjoying the sumptuous offerings of fresh fruit and a wide array of breakfast goodies. We shared a table with an Irish chap who was quite entertaining telling us of his travails over the Northern Route (*Camino del Norte*). When we finished eating, we returned to the room and readied ourselves for the day's activities.

Just before 10 am, we walked over to the Pilgrim's Office on *Rua Vilar* and lined up to received our *Compostelas* (Official Certificates of Completion). Directly behind us were two bicyclists who had biked the *Camino del Norte*. They were from Utah. One of the guys had previously lived in Northern Spain while he was completing his Mormon mission several years ago. It was interesting to get their perspective of what it was like biking the Camino. As it turned out, they were able to answer a lot of questions Heather and I had asked ourselves while we were walking regarding where they stayed, how many miles they covered per day, and things of that nature. Talking with them and sharing our experiences made the line move more quickly it seemed, and we were soon at the front. Leaving the Pilgrim's Office, we ran into Vince and Henrietta from Australia! Great to see them. They were staying at a hotel at the other side of town. We said goodbye and gave them a big hug. Also standing in line was the German couple whom we had met at *Casa Domingo* for lunch a few days back.

While shopping the day before, Heather had spotted a colorful purse/bag that she wanted to buy, so we found that shop and obtained the bag. Then she put the *"tubo"* that contained our *compostelas* in the newly acquired purse and we headed to the Cathedral early so we could get a good seat for the Pilgrim's Mass that was scheduled for 12 noon. Realizing we had plenty of time, we toured some of the more interesting parts of the Cathedral including the statue of St James and the "crypt" underneath. After spending some time looking at several of the small "chapels" that line the sides of the Cathedral, we proceeded over to the main seating area and quietly tried to position ourselves near the side by the massive columns so we could obtain a seat as soon as the current mass was completed.

To my surprise, I noticed that the *tirobolieros (six monks)* were getting in place to swing the *Botafumiero (the massive incense holder)*. I nudged Heather and made her aware of this then pulled out my smart phone to get a video of the entire event. Not long after, we were leaving the Cathedral and spending an hour or so shopping for gifts for our friends and loved ones along the busy *Rua Vilar* and all the shops near the *Plaza Quintana* and *Rua Azabacheria*.

We went back to the hotel and Heather took a long nap. I went outside and sat on the wall facing the north doors of the cathedral and just watched pilgrims come into the area for the first time. A concert was just starting up in the plaza right next to the hotel, so I stayed and watched that for awhile.

When I got back to the room, Heather was still sleeping, so I crawled into my bed and caught some shut-eye. When we woke up, we walked over to a restaurant I had eaten at last trip to get an early dinner, but it was unfortunately closed for the day. So we did some more shopping and then went back and ate dinner at the hotel.

Camino No. 1 – Day 39, Santiago de Compostela

The following morning there were more tourists who came up to us and said that they had heard about us and wanted to congratulate us for completing the Camino and wanted to hear more about it. It was somewhat embarrassing to us, but we did the best we could. Richard and Norma came in to eat, as did Sister Carol. We went back to the room and discussed whether or not we should get the bus to *Finesterre*. Ultimately, we thought this might be too much of a rush at the last minute, and if there was a delay of some sort, it might cause us to miss our plane to *Madrid*.

We got our bags packed and ready to go and checked them with the desk so that was off our minds. The clerk said that she would call us a cab to the airport whenever we wanted and that it would be 18 Euros and would take half an hour to get there. That gave us some peace of mind knowing that it was taken care of.

Then we left and went back to the Cathedral area for some additional shopping. It was a beautiful day once again, so we decided to walk up to *Santa Susanna* in the *Alameda Parque* at the west of town. There was an old Romanesque church there and a statue of *Rosalia de Castro*, a famous local poet.

This was a beautiful Sunday morning and the park and the streets were full of families really enjoying the day. Back near the Cathedral we sat for awhile between the police headquarters and the *Parador Hotel* and just looked at the Cathedral and its splendor.

In the square, there were still many pilgrims re-uniting for who knew how long and we rejoiced along with them at their joy in completing the trip as well as seeing old and new friends once again. We ate some nuts while sitting there in the warm sunshine, and then went back towards *Rua Vilar* and snapped some additional pictures.

Our friend with the sitar was set up and playing once again. Our plane did not leave until 5:40 so we still had a considerable amount of time before we need to be back to the hotel to catch the cab. We found the Cathedral museum near the spot where we received our *compostelas* and went inside to check that out. We were told that it would close within the hour, and so we made a rushed tour of the three-story building. There were some interesting artifacts and sculptures inside that we wished we could have had more time viewing. After a while we found a restaurant and ate our last meal. Appropriately, I decided on a Spanish omelet and a beer.

When we stepped outside we were surprised to see the blister expert we had encountered in *Sahagun* (from Seattle), and Elsa from Denmark (whom we had met in *Molinaseca*). We hugged each other, happy that we had all made it. A block or so away, we ran into Robert (Ghandi Ji) who told us he was getting ready to leave on the *Camino Portuguese*. His wife would join him from Australia, and they would walk a considerable portion together. After wandering the streets for another hour or so, we stopped at an ATM to get some cash, and then headed back to the hotel to wait there.

In the bar at the hotel, we ran into Richard and Norma once again and it was good to see them before we left. We exchanged email addresses and business cards. Norma asked us to share our spiritual experiences of the trip. I told her I just wasn't ready to do that since it had not all sunk in yet. We said goodbye and walked upstairs to the lobby to get the cab and go to the airport.

The ride to the airport was indeed only 20 minutes, and the driver dropped us off in the departure area. When we went inside to check our bags, we found out that we had missed our plane. The flight had been moved up to 3:00 and there were no more planes to *Madrid* that day! The Iberian Airlines representative told us we could get an early flight to *Madrid* in the morning that would still easily connect us with our flight to Dallas from there. So, it was not a disaster, but we would have to spend another night in *Santiago*. It was too late to cancel our room at the *Madrid* hotel for the evening, so we would just have to eat that. The airline rep recommended two hotels near the airport that were not very expensive, so we got a cab and went to the *Hotel Garcas*, only a five-minute ride from the airport. I asked the cab to wait while I checked to see if there was a room available. There was, and we paid the cab and checked in. *Garcas* was not unlike many of the places we had stayed at. The Wi-Fi only worked in the lobby/bar area so we posted our delay, which wasn't really a delay I suppose, just more of a change. We sat at the bar and had a few drinks. Dinner was not until 8:30, so Greg and I just ate some nuts and ice cream from the vending machine and went up to bed since we had to be up early.

Camino No. 2 – Day 19, Santiago de Compostela

Today was literally a walk in the park. At breakfast we were surprised by the German couple that we had met while eating lunch at Casa Domingo. They were so happy to see us and treated us like long, lost friends. This was so typical of the many Camino "friendships" we experienced over the days we were walking. We said our goodbyes with big hugs and kisses, realizing that we would most likely never see them again, ever. Heather had not been feeling particularly well, with a small Lupus onset, so we decided yesterday not to take the bus to Finisterre and just to remain in town and relax before the taxing trip home to the States. Yesterday, Heather had made an appointment at a local tattoo parlor to get a special, permanent souvenir of her trip. At 10:30, we walked over to the parlor and she got inked up. The image she used was the Logrono shell symbol that she had embellished with a cross. The entire process took less than an hour and it was altogether a very pleasant experience. We then wrapped up some remaining shopping errands, ate a snack at the hotel, and took off through the busy streets and into *Santa Susana* park where we sat for awhile and enjoyed the beautiful weather.

Later, back at the hotel, we both took long naps, and then packed up our gear to be ready at the crack of dawn to head for the airport. I went down to the desk to have them order a taxi pickup for us at 6:30 am. This is always a time of conflicting emotions, of course. Glad to be going home and sad to leave the wonderful experience behind. Heather said she was most looking forward to hearing English again and to see our dog, Stogie.

At dinner that evening, we saw the Germans we had met on the way down from *Cruz de Ferro*, the ones who had given Heather the salve made from Calendula flowers. Again, more hugs and kisses from relative strangers, and a little bit of nostalgia on our part, realizing that we had made many friends along the way and were feeling the regrets that, if we could, we would have enjoyed extending those encounters into long, lasting relationships. After dinner, Heather went back to the room and I went outside to get some night-time photos of the Cathedral, the surroundings and the great hallways of our hotel.

Chapter Sixteen

Going Home

Camino No. 1 – Day 40

We got out on time in the morning and caught a bus to the airport after waiting out on the main road for about a half hour. The flight to Madrid lasted about as long as it would take to fly to LA from Sacramento, and we arrived with plenty of time to change planes and get to Dallas on schedule.

Before we could move on to the gate, we were called into another security check. This turned out to be an interview. The security people split Greg and I up, and we were taken to different locations and questioned extensively. What were we doing in Spain? Why were we there for so long? Who had we contacted there? Had anyone else had access to our luggage in the last 24 hours? That sort of thing. I was finished within 5 minutes, and when they released me, I could not find Greg. I moved on to the Gate Area thinking I would see him there, but still no sight of him. In another 5 minutes, he finally showed up, smiling and shrugging his shoulders and laughing about the "incident." By this time, the plane was getting ready to board, so we got up to get in line for priority boarding. At that point, an airline official announced over the loudspeaker for Greg to report to the desk at the gate. He was being requested to submit to more questioning. A security official was waiting at the desk and escorted Greg away back through the terminal towards the area in which we had been previously questioned. I was not sure what to do at this point, because they had already begun boarding the plane. I watched Greg disappear down the concourse, so I stepped out of line for priority boarding and decided to wait until the last minute to get on the plane. As the next groups were called to board, there was still no sign of Greg, but he finally appeared as the final group was called up. He had no explanation for this except for the fact that they kept asking him additional questions about his original answers to their interview. He also thought that his name might be on some sort of "watch list" because he had similar things happen in the past. I was glad to be getting on the plane and thankful that I was not going to have to tell Marianne that he had been detained in Europe at Barajas International Airport!

We both tried unsuccessfully to sleep on the plane, and Greg was still suffering from a lingering cold that he had been dealing with now for well over a week. A Spanish girl was seated next to me, and I engaged her in some small talk. Her English was somewhat limited, but I asked here if she could translate a sign I had seen in *Ambasmestas*. She was unable to do so, indicating that it was a dialect with which she was unfamiliar. I thanked her anyway and then tried to get back to sleep. The rest of the flight was relatively uneventful and they fed us twice.

In Dallas, they kept changing the gates on us, and we had to even change terminals once, but we did have time to get a cheeseburger and fries in a restaurant there and call Heather and Marianne. Finally, we boarded the plane and landed in Sacramento right on time. The welcoming committee consisted of Heather, Marianne and Greg's son Stephen. They had made a big sign on top of a painting I had done last year of a kilometer marker (bollard) on the Camino. I hugged Heather until I think she could no longer breathe. It was so good to be back home in the arms of love.

Camino No. 2 – Day 20

The taxi was waiting outside the front door of *Hospederia San Martin Pinerio* at 6:30. We hopped in with our gear and directed the driver to take us to the airport. It was interesting to drive through the city in darkness, and we both noticed how beautifully it was lit up. By the time we reached the airport, it was light. We were both feeling sad that we would be leaving in a couple of hours, but still anxious to get home. We checked in at Iberia Air and spent a little time watching the shrink wrap operation before going through security and heading towards our gate. Heather saved a table for us and I went through the cafeteria line and got some breakfast items for us. When we had finished eating, we got a seat near our gate and waited for the flight to be called up.

After an hour or so, we got in line to board and began a conversation with a Danish woman in front of us who was intrigued by Heather's scarf. She wound up sitting next to us on the plane and we continued the conversation all the way to Madrid. When we got off the plane, it seemed as if we had to walk the entire length of T4 to get to the airport shuttle that took us to the other terminal where our US Airways plane was docked. To get to the boarding area we had to go through another passport control and questioning protocol. Then it was about an hour before we could board the plane.

The trip to Charlotte was relatively uneventful. I was able to watch 3 movies on my seat-back video screen, while Heather watched some TV shows and a couple of other movies. The airline served us two meals that were not too bad actually.

We arrived on time in Charlotte, NC and proceeded to the customs control and waited in line to get our passport stamped. Then we picked up our bags and transferred them to the connecting flights desk. Upstairs, I exchanged the last of my Euros at the kiosk, and then we wound our way to the gate to catch our flight to Sacramento. Not too long after, we were ready to board, and this is when the trouble began. After sitting on the plane for half an hour, the pilot announced that there was trouble with a couple of the warning lights that was preventing them from taking off until that problem was sorted out. A large groan emitted from all the passengers. After sitting on the plane for more than an hour, they finally announced that they could not fix the issue, and that we would all have to de-board the plane, and they would have another flight for us.

Two hours later, at the other end of the airport, we finally got on a new plane and settled in for the flight home. Needless to say, everyone was tired and irritable by this time. Before getting on the plane, I called my friend Norm who was going to pick us up at Sacramento airport and updated him on the status of the flight. I told him that we could get a taxi home, if it was getting too late for him, but he insisted that he would be there, no matter what the time. Great to have friends like this! My memory is hazy about this last leg of the trip, but I think they served us more food and drink. At Sacramento airport, we arrived during a late-night security drill which had the place locked down tightly except for our flight. Heather found Norm outside at arrivals and I waited for our bags to come in on the conveyor belt. An hour later we were home safely. I calculated that from the time we got on the taxi in Santiago until walking into our house, it was 27 hours! Whew!

Our dog, Stogie, was overjoyed to see us, so we spent some time playing with him, then had a bowl of cereal before crawling into bed. Tomorrow we would begin the re-entry process. As anyone who has made a trip of this sort knows, we were drained, emotionally and physically — filled with gratitude that we were home safely, but also feeling melancholy that we would not be walking the next day to a new exciting location.

Epilogue

I have come to realize that returning home and getting back to your "routine" can be as much of a culture shock as starting that first day of your walk from wherever that may have been. In fact, from my perspective, this topic is *enormous*. In varying degrees, you will find that you will have been unalterably changed by the Camino experience.

I have found that many pilgrims are unable to put their finger on the change that has occurred right away. It may take weeks or months or even years to come to grips with what has happened. But it seems fairly universal that, after a time, most of us long to be back on the Camino, and we seek to encapsulate that longing – only to find that this is usually quite difficult.

We want to share the experience with our family and friends, but we are saddened by the bittersweet fact that they might not be as interested in what we have to say as we are excited to share it – if that makes sense! I think this is why Camino social media sites, like APOC, are so popular now. Everyone on those sites really gets it. We share pictures, stories and are so happy to help others struggling on the Camino or preparing to go and have thousands of questions – just like we did when we set out!

On my first Camino, I had hoped to journal my experiences every day, but quite honestly, I was too tired at the end of the day to accomplish this. It was all I could do to handle/wash my gear, communicate with my family back home (which I had promised to do), clean up, bandage and manage my blisters, find a place to eat and get some sleep. In the early parts, I tried to journal, but found myself falling asleep soon after trying and after a week or so, I just gave up.

Six months after returning, I set up a blog site using WordPress and began to blog of these experiences and included pictures of the trip. This eventually turned into a large project and bled over into my second Camino with Heather. I called the blog *My Senior Camino*, and you can google that to get a different presentation with lots of pictures. My intentions in writing the blog in the first place were to (1) preserve the memories and experiences for myself and (2) to share the experience with others. I have been quite gratified by all the response I have had to this blog over the years, and many have encouraged me to write a book about it. I vacillated over and over about this for months, but finally got to work and accomplished it.

The *Camino de Santiago Forum* has named *My Senior Camino* one of the "Top 17 for 2015", and as recently at February 2017 is still being cited as one of the top blogs. It is a great honor to be included in that group! Since the blog was started, there have been over 3,850 visitors and nearly 15,000 views from 93 countries around the world. These range from the United States to China, and include such diverse places as Pakistan, Bangladesh, Botswana, United Arab Emirates, Maldives, Sri Lanka and Qatar. After the USA, the most visitors have come from Australia, Brazil, Canada and the United Kingdom.

I am sure that there are innumerably more sites about the *Camino de Santiago* that have garnered far more interest than this one, but nonetheless, I am extremely gratified that this humble travelogue (and that is what it is) has provided some small amount of pleasure and information about walking the Camino, especially for those of you who are, shall we say, "up in years."

It was this response that prompted me to begin the project of making this travelogue from the blog into a book that one might be able to access more readily, shall we say. In the last ten years, more and more seniors are "retiring" from full-time work and looking for adventure. These are the "boomers," and they are not content to be sitting at home. I met a lot of them on my two Caminos. My experience has shown me that these "older" *peregrinos* are desirous of using their resources wisely and planning ahead to get the most out of their experience. I hope this book serves that purpose in some small way.

One thing, for sure. You will continue to have recollection upon recollection and be bathed in fond memories, hopefully forever. When we have the opportunity to share these recollections, it is a wonderful blessing. Here's one that I had:

Heather and I were walking along the *rio Pereje*, crossing back and forth over the busy N-IV for nearly two hours before coming into the tiny village of *Pereje*. Heather noticed a small church just off the street that looked interesting and indicated that she wanted to stop and take a look. The doors were open and candles were lit in the small chapel. We stopped for a moment, left a small donation, signed the guest book and received a *sello* from the host in our *credentiales*. As we were leaving to get back on the trail, I noticed a fellow pilgrim with a heavily bandaged leg struggling to make his way down the four steps at the front of the church. I stepped forward and took his arm and helped him down. He could hardly walk but managed to right himself at the bottom of the steps. We chatted briefly and he thanked me profusely for helping him. We said *"buen Camino"* and bid farewell. The following morning, as we were getting ready to leave, we saw the young man at the same pension where we stayed the night. He had been joined by his father and two others who were all walking. He introduced himself as Thiago, from *Brazilia, Brazil*. Thiago said he felt a little better this morning, but he was walking very slowly. He was determined to make it to *Santiago* however. We then met the rest of the group, wished each other well, and headed out.

Two days later, as we were leaving Samos in a drizzling rain, we once again ran into Thiago. He had gotten a little stronger, but was still limping along. We saw him the next day also, and were able to walk with him a bit. He told us of his life in *Brazilia*. He was 30 years old, the same age as our son Dylan, and had a wife back home who was pregnant and about ready to deliver. Because of her condition, she was unable to walk the Camino, so Thiago's father took her place. He was anxious to finish the Camino and get back to her. The three of us talked for about an hour or so. We learned that Thiago was a devout

Catholic and a very gentle soul. We had an immediate connection and were sad to part ways.

Weeks later, when I was compiling the diary of our trip, I posted this recollection on the blog. Thiago, already back in Brazil by this time, saw the post and wrote a comment to me:

"My pleasure to meet you at the Camino. Never forget our first meeting, in the way from VilaFranca for Las Herrerias, when my problems with blisters and tendinitis started. I was trying to leave a small church which had only three steps in front of it and I almost couldn't go down there. So you came and helped me. That's the magic about the Camino. A small act like this, helping somebody to walk only three steps, it's the only necessary thing to be forever thankful for someone and to never forget someone's face. Thank you, my friend, and Buen Camino...Thiago"

Eugene Petersen's book *A Long Obedience in the Same Direction* has long been a very influential work for me, and I continue to revisit it on a regular basis. It is a wonderful study of the *Songs of Ascent* which are the psalms numbered 120 through 134 in the book of Psalms. These 15 psalms were likely sung by Hebrew pilgrims as they went "up to Jerusalem" to the great worship festivals.

Petersen points out that Jerusalem was the highest point geographically in Palestine, so the pilgrims spent most of their time physically "ascending;" however, Petersen tells us that the trip was not only literal, but metaphorical as well. So, in that sense, the pilgrims, in going up to Jerusalem, were also acting out a life lived upward toward God. The pilgrims were remembering what God had done for them, as they had been commanded to do in the Scriptures. They were "refreshing their memories of God's saving ways", as Petersen puts it. Making these trips four times a year from their tribal communities to gather with the whole nation of Israel to worship and give thanks also served to let younger generations know that they were part of something much larger–an important concept in discipleship.

Peterson refers to this a metaphor as "an existence that advanced from one level to another in developing maturity." He tells us that this is what the Apostle Paul described as "the upward call of God in Christ Jesus" (Phil. 3:14).

Peterson tells us that William Faulkner, the American novelist, brilliantly described the Psalms of Ascents in this manner:

"They are not monuments, but footprints. A monument only says, 'At least I got this far,' while a footprint says, 'This is where I was when I moved again.'"

As I look back and remember my 500-mile trek along the Camino Frances, I find that I have a constant "longing" to be back there, a "yearning" to be focused on nothing but the day's walk without the clutter of everyday stuff that I find stifling. I miss the joy of experiencing new things at every turn of the road, meeting new people continually, and confronting the physical, mental and spiritual challenges every step of the way.

Remember, it bears repeating that when you get up in the morning, you step outside, turn to the West and keep walking until you stop for the day. Along the way you enjoy everything and everyone you encounter. Then you get up and do it again, and again and again. I long to live this way every day.

I now understand that this is what the Camino teaches us. We can, and should, be on that road all the time. Regardless of our own unique personalities, our cultural or ethnic heritages, our religious or socio-political differences, which can create giant chasms, we are all better people when we learn to live in community — sharing our common experiences and then celebrating our differences. We may not agree on everything in a worldly sense, but it is possible to obtain clarity and practice intellectual honesty as we move through life together.

When I returned home after my first Camino, I sifted through my memorabilia and came across the card that Sister Carol had given me in the hotel bar in Santiago. She had obtained it at *Santa Maria a Real do Cebriero*, a beautiful old church that I was too tired to find at the end of the day. I keep it in a prominent place and remember it often. It is simply called *Pilgrims Prayer*. Here it is:

*"Although I may have traveled all the roads, crossed mountains and valleys from East to West, if I have not discovered the freedom to be myself, **I have arrived nowhere.***

*Although I may have shared all of my possessions with people of other languages and cultures; made friends with Pilgrims of a thousand paths, or shared albergue with saints and prices, if I am not capable of forgiving my neighbor tomorrow, **I have arrived nowhere**.*

*Although I may have carried my pack from beginning to end and waited for every Pilgrim in need of encouragement, or given my bed to one who arrived later than I, given my bottle of water in exchange for nothing; if upon returning to my home and work, I am not able to create brotherhood or to make happiness, peace and unity, **I have arrived nowhere***

*Although I may have had food and water each day, and enjoyed a roof and shower every night; or may have had my injuries well attended, if I have not discovered in all that the love of God, **I have arrived nowhere.***

*Although I may have seen all the monuments and contemplated the best sunsets; although I may have learned a greeting in every language, or tasted the clean water from every fountain; if I have not discovered who is the author of so much free beauty and so much peace, **I have arrived nowhere**.*

*If from today I do not continue walking on your path searching and living according to what I have learned; if from today I do not see in every person, friend or foe a companion on the Camino; if from today I cannot recognize God, the God of Jesus of Nazareth as the one God of my life, **I have arrived nowhere."***

Finally, some parting words from Thoreau:

"So we saunter toward the Holy Land, till one day the sun shall shine more brightly than ever he has done, shall perchance shine into our minds and hearts, and light up our whole lives with a great awakening light, as warm and serene and golden as on a bankside in autumn"

Get out and walk, seniors! It is the best thing you can do for your body and mind!

Made in the USA
Coppell, TX
28 February 2021